KV-374-143

CONTENTS

World in Transformation

LATIN AMERICA

by

F J Poppleton

Ginn and Company Ltd

18 Bedford Row
London WC1R 4EJ

ACKNOWLEDGEMENTS

We are grateful to the following for permission to reproduce the photographs in this book:
The American Museum of Natural History (p. 25); Camera Press Ltd., (pp. 77, lower and 110, lower); Compania Mexicana Aerofoto (p. 11, upper); ex-Convento de Julhuacan, Mexico (p. 121); Charles Gibson, *Spain in America*, Harper and Row (p. 41); S. D. Madariaga, *Bolivar*, University of Miami Press (p. 60); Manchete Press Agency, Río de Janeiro (p. 152); Mansell Collection (p. 89); Janet Poppleton (pp. 4, 18 and facing pp. 32, 33, 64, 65, 96, 97, 128 and 129); Radio Times Hulton Picture Library (p. 77, upper); Städtische Kunsthalle, Mannheim (p. 91); and United Press International (p. 110, upper and p. 132).

The maps and tables are by E. Mudge-Marriott. The figures in tables A and B on page 147 and in the cost of living tables on page 149 are from the United Nations Monthly Bulletin of Statistics, April 1970, and in table C on page 147, from the United Nations Statistical Bulletin for Latin America, 1968; for the racial composition tables, from D. D. Brand, *Some Educational and Anthropological Aspects of Latin America*, Austin, Texas. The figures in the tables of education on page 149 are from Unesco (B and C) and *Latin America: Handbooks to the Modern World* series, ed. C. Veliz, Anthony Blond (A). The figures for the trade tables on page 151 are from International Financial Statistics, July 1968 and March 1969.

The reconstruction drawing on page 10 is by Martin Simmons.

© F. J. Poppleton 1971   107104   ISBN 0 602 21166 2

Phototypeset by Oliver Burridge Filmsetting Ltd., Crawley, Sussex

Printed in Great Britain by Fletcher & Son Ltd., Norwich

CHAPTER ONE
The setting

Latin America embraces twenty republics. They may be divided into three separate groups: ten in South America—Argentina, Bolivia, Brazil, Chile, Colombia, Ecuador, Paraguay, Peru, Uruguay and Venezuela; seven in North and Central America—Mexico, Costa Rica, El Salvador, Guatemala, Honduras, Nicaragua, and Panama; three in the Caribbean—Cuba, the Dominican Republic, and Haiti. Nineteen of the twenty states were colonies of Spain and Portugal for three hundred years and have been strongly influenced by their Iberian heritage. The exception, Haiti, was a French colony from 1697 until independence in 1803, and it is still French speaking.

Latin America is the most accurate simple term to use to describe these twenty states. Latin America covers an area of about 13 million square kilometres equalling that of Europe and the United States combined. South America stretches 9,600 kilometres from north to south, and at its widest is about half that distance. Most of the countries lie completely within the tropics. Of the others, a small part of Brazil, half of Paraguay and the greater parts of both Argentina and Chile lie in the temperate zones. Only one state, Uruguay, is situated entirely outside the tropics. Although the majority of Latin Americans live within the tropics, many populated areas are situated so high above sea level that the altitude seriously modifies the climate.

Much of the mountain chain stretching from the United States border with Mexico to the southern tip of Chile cannot be cultivated because of poor soils, oppressive climate and rugged terrain. Large areas of northern Mexico, the Peruvian and Chilean coasts, southern Argentina and north-east Brazil are too dry for agriculture.

Only one of the four large river basins, the Río de la Plata, has been developed to any extent. The others, the basins of the rivers Amazon, Orinoco and Magdalena, contain badly leached soils which are infertile. Although Latin America is rich in minerals of all kinds, many of them are too inaccessible or too expensive to extract. The mountainous character of the continent has made the development of land communications difficult. For this reason air transport is now more important to Latin America than to any other world region.

Races

Life in the Andes is still carried out in the time-honoured pattern first established by the Incas. Despite centuries of Iberian influence, the Indian and negro cultures remain vigorous and important. In 1966 it was estimated that there were 20 million Indians and 25 million negroes in Latin America out of a total population of 244 million. The Indians speak their own languages and most of them remain unassimilated in Latin American society. They form large numbers in the populations of Bolivia, Peru, Ecuador, Guatemala and Mexico. They remain, after four hundred years of foreign rule, culturally separate from white society, even if subject to its laws.

The negroes brought from Africa as slaves constitute a large and important element in the populations of the countries which fringe the Caribbean, especially Haiti, and Brazil. The negro in Brazil has been absorbed by intermarriage, and the country is the only true 'melting pot' of races in the world, but the negro influence here is still strong, especially in Brazilian music and literature. The annual carnivals in Brazil bear testimony to her African heritage.

The Indians and the negroes provided women for the European invaders. Their children were called 'mestizos' and 'mulatos', meaning a mixture of white and Indian, and white and negro respectively. Some countries in the Caribbean and notably Paraguay in South America have predominantly mestizo populations. Haiti, in the Caribbean, is an example of a country with a mulato population.

Between 1860 and 1930 the former colonial powers of Spain and

**States and capitals
of Latin America**

Portugal sent a new mass of settlers to Latin America, totalling many millions. Italians also emigrated in large numbers especially to Uruguay, Argentina and Chile where names like Alessandri and Frondizi remind one of their successful settlements. During the nineteenth century settlers from Northern Europe arrived in the states which had gained independence. Small in numbers but often highly skilled, they helped to modernise Brazil, Uruguay, Argentina and Chile, supported by British capital investment. In the twentieth century the United States has taken on the mantle of the British investors, and Latin America is now closely linked to the United States economy. Despite all these non-Latin influences, however, the most pervasive remains that of Spain and Portugal.

Myth and reality

The twenty republics vary in climate and relief and in their traditions, languages and race. It is misleading to think of a Latin American 'type' or a Latin American 'reaction'. In the Anglo-Saxon world the average Latin American has been traditionally seen as an emotional, flamboyant person, preoccupied with football and politics. He has been thought to be ruled by military dictators notorious for their inefficiency and corruption. His life has been assumed to be one of unceasing labour, working under hot sun in the open fields of a 'hacienda', or plantation. It would be difficult to find either such a pattern of life or such a Latin American today. Most Latin Americans live in cities whose average temperatures rarely exceed those of western Europe. Some of the largest cities in the world are found in the region. Buenos Aires boasts over 6 million, Mexico City, Río de Janeiro and São Paulo number 5 million, and at least six other cities have over 1 million inhabitants.

The idea persists that Latin America is politically unstable. In comparison with Africa and Asia this is untrue. Even in western Europe few countries can look back on long periods of unbroken constitutional or democratic government. Few states in the world could match the political stability of Chile and Brazil in the nineteenth century, or the record of free elections and democratic rule of Uruguay and Costa Rica in the twentieth century. The military leaders of Latin America are now more often than not to be found supporting civilian reformers and not preserving unrepresentative landowners, as in the nineteenth century. Only a few old-style dictators survive, and none of them rule major countries. They have been replaced by political parties of a progressive blend which are determined to carry out changes in the social pattern.

The standard of living of Latin Americans compares very favourably with that of Africans or Asians. As a region Latin America occupies a midway position between the Afro-Asian 'bloc' and the sophisticated Western nations. Many of its cultural and social patterns reflect those of Europe and North America, while its economic problems seem to be those of an underdeveloped area.

Three of the most urgent problems now facing Latin America are: how to control population and increase food supply; how to diversify the economy and develop internationally viable industries; and how to improve both the quantity and quality of education. The transition of Latin America from her present position to one of greater sophistication depends on successful answers to these questions.

*The present day site of Teotihuacán, above,
and below, a reconstruction of Tenochtitlán*

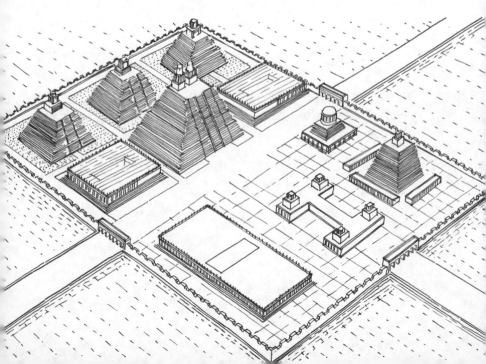

CHAPTER TWO

The Pre-Columbian civilisations

The most widely accepted theory of the origins of human life on the American continent is that hunters and fishermen moved westward from the Old World via the Bering Straits. Hunters were active on the plains of North America by the year 10,000 BC, and they pressed down along the eastern edge of the Rocky Mountains into Mexico. From there they moved into the rest of Latin America. Archaeological finds prove the presence of human beings by 10,000 BC in Mexico and by 7,000 BC on the edge of the Magellan Straits. These hunters spread into areas where big game hunting was impossible, and to survive they had to extend their range of food to plants. Maize was developed in the desert areas of the south western United States and its domestication was the first step in the development of settled communities. Two thousand BC marked the domestication of maize in Mexico and thereafter all the civilisations in Mexico and Central America, which is called Meso America, and the Andes depended on it.

In the 3,600 years following the first settlement of Mexico many great cultures rose and fell, of which three, the Aztec, the Maya of Meso America, and the Inca of the Andes, were the most significant. These cultures reached a high level of development while a few primitive people like the Ona of the Magellan Straits remain at the simple level of those first inhabitants, the hunters even today.

Mexico (1500 BC-AD 600)

In Mexico there were many dominant groups before the Aztecs. Farmers settled in the rich Valley of Mexico in the second millenium BC. This valley was the cradle and the continuing centre of development from this time forward. Situated near the southern edge of the mesa central, it extends approximately 120 kilometres in a north-south direction and 65 kilometres from east to west. Technically it is not a valley but a basin for it lacks a natural outlet. Volcanic eruption beginning in the late tertiary period gave it the form of an irregular elliptical depression surrounded by high mountains. It lies equidistant between the Pacific and the Caribbean.

Villages supported themselves during the second millenium by growing maize and other vegetables. Pottery and simple tools of stone, bone and wood were made and used. This early society was dominated by religion, and a great city was built in the north-east corner of the Valley of Mexico, called Teotihuacán.

Teotihuacán was built and rebuilt at least three times between 100 BC and AD 600, each time more elaborately than the last. At its greatest extent it covered eleven square kilometres, and perhaps as many as 50,000 people lived there. During the years of its existence cultural life developed considerably. The decorated pottery and designed frescoes from the end of the period contrast strongly with the simple artefacts which had been in use at the beginning. By the end of the sixth century AD public buildings had replaced adobe huts, and terraced pyramids lined the long central avenue which formed its main artery, for Teotihuacán was a religious centre for the people living in the Valley of Mexico.

Mexico: Toltec civilisation (AD 600-1100)

Teotihuacán was destroyed about AD 600, and though its situation made it an obvious target for attack, the actual details of its destruction are unknown. A confused period followed. Warriors from the north, called Toltecs, established control in the Valley of Mexico and built a centre at Tula, north-west of Teotihuacán. The Toltecs absorbed the culture of Teotihuacán, and introduced new practices into the religion, including the worship of the feathered serpent called Quetzalcoátl.

They, in turn, lost control of the Valley of Mexico about 1100, and for two hundred years, until about 1325, rival tribes fought for leadership. The Aztec civilisation was to emerge from this anarchy as a mixture of the cultures of different tribes.

The areas controlled by the Toltecs, Aztecs and Mayas at the height of their power

- Mayas circa 550
- Toltecs circa 950
- Aztecs circa 1500

0   500
Kilometres

Aztec Civilisation (1300-1521)

One of these tribes, the Tenochas, who came to be known as the Aztecs, occupied islands in the lakes of the Valley of Mexico in order to escape extermination at the hands of the other tribes. The Aztecs gained dominance over the Valley after a century-long struggle, and built a centre there, Tenochtitlán, the forerunner of Mexico City, which in 1429 became the Aztec capital.

The amalgam of cultural ideas and traditions which made up the Aztec civilisation produced a loose, ever-changing society. It was originally a simple and democratic society, but, as it developed, it became more hierarchical and class conscious. It established a communal tradition which survives to this day in the 'ejidos', or communal lands. In contrast to both the Inca and the Maya civilisations, the Aztecs placed great emphasis on service and obtaining high rank through effort.

In order to understand the Aztec civilisation one must realise the importance of religion. For the Aztecs religion meant the worship of the forces of nature and the supernatural. The priests tried to win the support of favourable gods, and to repel harmful forces by a ritual which involved human sacrifices. This macabre situation was accepted quite naturally; the way the priests interpreted the portents was not questioned by the people. The gods all had a special significance. Many were associated with fertility and the elements, such as the Rain God, Taloc. One of the most important gods was Quetzalcoátl, the feathered serpent and god of civilisation, who had, they believed, once ruled the Toltecs and would someday return from the east by sea. There was an incessant demand for sacrificial victims, and the gods demanded the most precious part of the human body, the heart. This ritual part of Aztec religion was the cause of continual wars, and when peace reigned special combats were staged to satisfy the demands of the priests.

If Aztec civilisation was dominated by religion, it was obsessed by war. Every boy was trained in school to use weapons and was expected to fight when the need arose. Yet the military machine which had forged an Empire stretching from Guatemala to the Tropic of Cancer ultimately had no chance against European soldiery.

The communities which made up the Aztec Empire were self-governing, but matters affecting groups of communities were settled by representative councils. These councils appointed one chief to control civil and religious matters, and another for war. The men who ruled were able: they had reached their posts as administrators through effort and ability. Besides administration three other careers were highly valued—trades, craft and religion.

The Aztec system was maintained by strict laws. If people did not play their part in the community they could lose their citizenship, and this meant that they became slaves. The severity of the laws can be best judged by listing five crimes and punishments:

to pilfer in the market meant instant death by stoning;

to steal corn meant death by slavery;
to be drunk meant stoning or beating to death;
to impersonate an official meant death;
to slander meant to have's one's lips and ears cut off.

The system existed for the benefit of the healthy and able, but not for social misfits. Personal freedom was severely limited, and the resentment which resulted led to internal dissensions in the Empire. Moctezuma, the Aztec emperor, was stoned by his own people in 1519 after the arrival of Cortés. Yet this harsh system had worked continuously for over one hundred years.

Children were brought up to become adult as quickly as possible; for instance the education of boys was supervised by their fathers who taught them how to use tools and weapons. At the age of fifteen all boys were instructed in citizenship. After this some trained for religious duties in seminaries, some became soldiers; some became traders and artists.

Girls were trained in craftwork and household duties, but when they reached womanhood they gained certain important rights. They could help choose their husbands, and once married they could be freed if their husbands were cruel or failed to support them. Women also gained positions of prominence through acting as regents for men who were too young to assume chieftainships.

Agriculture was organised in a simple manner. Land was divided among families by the council, and sections were reserved to be worked communally as ejidos, for the maintenance of the chief and priests. This system worked well as long as the pressure of population on the land did not reach saturation level. Once this happened, conflict between communities resulted.

The breakdown of the system also led to emigration in search of new lands, and this explains in some measure the reasons for the expansion of the Aztec Empire from the Valley of Mexico to the forests of Guatemala in the south, and to the Pacific and Atlantic Oceans to the west and east. The Tenochans in the fourteenth century resolved their particular land shortage by creating islands of mud bound together by tree roots and reeds. These floating gardens exist today.

The Aztecs grew many foods which are now universally used, especially maize, tomatoes and beans. One bean, the cacao, was used for food (to make chocolate) and for trade. The Aztecs, like the Mayas before them and the Incas later, had no coinage, so they used cacao beans to balance any small inequality in their system of barter.

Aztec craftsmanship was highly skilled. This was especially apparent in the pottery, basketwork and carvings they produced. Much of it was inspired by religious sentiments. The Mayas had built up trade routes throughout Meso America and the Aztecs used them to trade with other parts of the continent. They traded mainly in handicrafts, tools, ornaments and pottery.

One further point about the Aztecs is important. The contemporary mediaeval European scale of values held no appeal for them. The evidence for this is that they esteemed jade and not gold, and they had no elaborate laws governing private property as the Europeans had.

The Mayas (AD c100-1200)

The Maya civilisation collapsed long before the arrival of the Spaniards. The Mayas were neither warriors like the Aztecs nor great Empire builders like the Incas, but rather a deeply religious and peace loving tribe. Their civilisation was mysterious, dominated by religion, yet without the cruel excesses of the Aztecs. Priests ruled everything and were preoccupied with studying astronomy, drawing up a 365-day calendar and perfecting a system of notation, comparable to the Arabic system. Hieroglyphics survive which recorded outstanding events, carefully dated according to the Maya calendar. Scholars disagree about how to interpret this calendar, but agree on both its accuracy and similarity to the Gregorian calendar, adopted at a later date in the West.

The Maya civilisation first developed in the rain forest on the borders of Guatemala. Its main crop was like that of the city of Teotihuacán, maize, cultivated in private and communal plots called 'milpas'. The Mayas did not conserve the soil in any way, but having exhausted it in one area, they shifted to another. This may not have been a very promising basis for an advanced community, yet the Mayas were certainly advanced. Their architecture was highly sophisticated. They built impressive temples atop pyramids in the middle of the jungle, and their cities were laid out in a series of squares and rectangles, surrounded by interlinking courtyards and priests' dwellings.

The first stage of Maya civilisation lasted from the beginning of the Christian era to about AD 700. The early cities then fell into decay while another civilisation developed on the limestone plateau of Yucatán in southern Mexico, two hundred and forty kilometres away to the north-east. This second stage lasted roughly from AD 700-1200. The cities that were built in this period (for example see Chichen Itza, map on page 13) were less impressive than those of the first, and show clear signs of foreign influence, especially from the Toltecs to the west. Why did this mass migration to the north-east take place? The question has never been satisfactorily answered. There is evidence that the move was planned rather than being the result of a sudden disaster. It is probable that soil exhaustion in the forests caused the move, for the Mayas found themselves clearing more and more jungle away from the villages to create new milpas. Hence a time would have arrived when a mass migration was both logical and realistic.

The second stage of Maya civilisation also ended in strange circumstances. One reason suggested for its decline is that Yucatán is a poor limestone plateau and soil exhaustion would have followed even more quickly under the milpas system. It was a difficult area to conquer. During the period of Spanish discovery Cortés spent six months hacking his way through the bush and jungle, only to find the cities in ruins, overrun by vegetation. There were no signs of a fight between the Mayas and any invaders; had they been attacked, the Mayas could have offered little resistance to the Toltecs, but the most likely explanation is that the population just declined.

Peru before the Incas (c1200 BC-AD c1400)

The early civilisation of South America reached its highest level in the Andean region and more particularly in Peru and Highland Bolivia. The beginnings of a settled agricultural life in the Andean

region probably dates from 1200 BC. The earliest known centre was in the Virú Valley to the north of Lima. The level of cultural achievements was similar to that of the first villages in Mexico. By the beginning of the Christian era communities had developed all along the Peruvian coast both north and south of the site where modern Lima stands. The two outstanding cultures in the period up to AD 800 were those of the Moche and the Nazca. Both produced arts and crafts which are world renowned. Moche pottery was beautifully designed, and the pictures painted on the vessels give a detailed commentary of the way of life of the Moche. The Paracas textiles represent the best known examples of Nazca achievement. Moche culture reached an advanced technical state, in some spheres, hardly bettered by the Incas. The early inhabitants of Peru were also successful agriculturalists. They developed beans, maize, potatoes, sweet potatoes and many of the tropical fruits which still colour market stalls in Peru. They were the first people to use the deposits of guano, found on the offshore islands of Peru, as a fertiliser. They also developed a system of irrigation.

Cultural advance in the Andes was slower, but between AD 800 and AD 1200 the highlands began to exercise an influence over the coastal area. The centre of this highland influence was Tiahuanaco, a city built at over 400 metres above sea level on the Bolivian plateau. Tiahuanaco was situated a short distance from Lake Titicaca and five kilometres from the quarries which provided the stone with which the city was built. It seems to have been a centre for religious ceremony not unlike Teotihuacán, and if the visitor to the site today is impressed by the ruins that remain, an Indian eight hundred years ago would have been overawed by the buildings, including the giant statues, which covered the area. Many of these have been removed but the illustration opposite shows the best remaining example at Tiahuanaco.

Extravagant claims have been made for Tiahuanaco culture—that it was the cradle of American or even world civilisation—but its influence lasted only for a brief period. Between about 1200 and 1400 regional cultures were again predominant, and one established at Cuzco about 1250, became the centre of the Inca civilisation.

Sculpture from the pre-Inca period at Tiahuanaco

Inca civilisation (1438–1532)

The Incas united into the greatest New World Empire an enormous area of territory from central Chile to the northern frontiers of Ecuador. The Empire covered about 500,000 square kilometres and stretched 3,300 kilometres from north to south. It was organised by provinces each with 200,000 people, and estimates of population put the total number of people at between 3·5 million and 7 million.

This empire was established by two outstanding rulers, Pachacuti Inca (1438-1471) and his son Topa Inca (1471-1493). Pachacuti has been described as the greatest man that the indigenous race of America produced, and the two together have been compared to Philip of Macedon and his son, Alexander the Great. Both men were exceptional military leaders as well as having outstanding ability in government. Pachacuti planned and built the city of Cuzco. He laid down the system of government of the Empire on a strictly hierarchical basis in which the Emperor was supreme. Topa's great achievement was the construction of the great fortress of Sacsahuaman, above Cuzco, which was one of the most impressive single examples of the work of Inca stonemasons.

With the death of Topa Inca the Empire had reached its apogee. There followed the rule of Huayna Capac (1493-1525), who faced ever growing internal problems. Upon his death the Empire was rent by civil war between two of his sons, Atahualpa and Huascar, which lasted until the arrival of Pizarro, and the Spanish 'conquistadores', or conquerors.

What had the Incas achieved in the one hundred years before their downfall? Their Empire had the most advanced political and social system in the New World. The picture that can be built up is of an Empire strictly organised and rigidly controlled.

The Inca language, Quechua, the Inca style of dress, and the official Sun-worshipping religion, were imposed on each newly acquired province. If any group rebelled whole villages were transferred to other parts of the Empire, to be replaced by reliable subjects whose loyalty was unquestioned. The Empire was linked by roads, and 'chasquis', or professional runners, who provided an efficient messenger service throughout the Empire. It is known, for

Caribbean Sea

SOUTH

Quito
Tumbez
R. Amazon
Cajamarca

AMERICA

Inca civilisation
CIRCA 1465

Cuzco
L.Titicaca
Tiahuanaco
Pacific
Ocean
CHILE

Full Inca control

Partial Inca control

0   1000
Kilometres

instance that fresh fish was brought by relays of runners from the coast to the capital within two days—a distance of 240 kilometres.

From Cuzco the Empire was governed by a ruler who was called Inca. (The word originally applied to a small group of families who had settled in the region of Cuzco, but came to mean all the peoples of the Empire.) He divided his lands into quarters, which were in turn subdivided into provinces, and further still into smaller units, the 'ayllu'. The ayllu was like a close knit village, and each one had its part to play in the imperial organisation. The population was classified into age groups to determine who should pay the taxes, the most important category being the able-bodied adults, aged from twenty-five to fifty years. These adults were given special tasks as labourers, builders, or soldiers, and records were kept of

21

their performances. Records were made in an ingenious and unique way. A series of strings, in which knots were tied, were attached to a main cord up to a yard long. This device was called a 'quipu', and no word can translate its meaning. The quipu recorded numbers by means of knots, and different products by means of coloured strings. The quipus varied greatly, and it is impossible to know exactly how they were interpreted. Special men were trained for this task by the Inca. A census of every new province was taken during the Inca period, and senior officials were brought in by the Incas from the capital to control affairs, though local junior officials remained in their positions.

The Incas developed a simple tax system: all land which could be cultivated was divided into three parts. The produce of the smallest area was assigned to support the priests; that of the largest was retained by the ayllu for its own support, and the third area provided for state officials and nobles. Careful records were kept of all production, and surplus stock was stored to provide relief in times of disaster. The flock of llamas and alpacas were sometimes owned by the state and sometimes by the individual ayllu.

This political and economic organisation is the aspect of the Inca civilisation which has been most widely commented on. No personal freedom existed either of movement or speech, but the state provided adequately for everyone. The Inca civilisation was certainly the first welfare state in the New World, but in other ways it was not remarkable. The level of artistic achievement never reached either that of Meso America or that of the Moche. Trade was much more limited than in Meso America because movement of the ordinary Indian from his ayllu was restricted. There was no coinage and the abundant metals available were used chiefly for religious motifs.

Religion never attained the same pre-eminent position in Inca life that it did under the Mayas or even the Aztecs. The Inca was thought to be descended from the sun and was regarded as someone who ruled by Divine Right. A state religion, Sun worship, was established throughout the Empire, but animals rather than human beings were the usual victims of sacrifice. Alongside this state religion older local fetishes flourished, as they still do today. The remarkable fact about these personal religions is that they absorbed and adapted Spanish Catholicism as surely as they had done Sun worship before.

The most notable technical achievement of the Incas was their building. Without advanced technological aids such as the wheel, they built massive structures. They worked both in rectangular shaped blocks and also in many sided irregular stones. Their workmanship has survived earthquakes over 600 years, while more recent buildings have been destroyed. The best surviving example of the Inca stonemasons' work can be seen in the ruins of Machu Picchu, a complete city still in remarkable condition. As civil engineers the Incas bear comparison with the Romans. Suspension bridges, aqueducts, and roads were constructed in mountains higher than any in Europe. The two main roads of the Empire ran for well over 3,200 kilometres each, from Ecuador in the north to Chile and Argentina in the south.

The best description of Inca rule is probably enlightened despotism. A dictatorship may be anathema to people brought up in a democratic tradition, but the Inca rule succeeded for one hundred years and provided security against disaster. If one looks at the Inca civilisation in the light of others in Latin America its greatness stands out. In the centuries since the fall of the Incas the Indians have been regimented and organised by Europeans or mestizos, who saw them merely as a race to be exploited, and only now are the Andean Indians recovering some of their dignity, lost four hundred years ago.

The three great Pre-Columbian civilisations in the New World have left a legacy. None could hope to survive the challenge of Western Europe, which was based on a more sophisticated technology, but their influences are still widespread. The traveller in Mexico or the Andes can see today how close this past is to the present and how little the life of the Indian changed as a result of the conquest.

CHAPTER THREE

Discovery and conquest (1492-1580)

The expansion of the European world had far reaching consequences. The Portuguese and Spaniards were active during the period now known as the Age of Discovery. Spain's main spheres of interest were Mexico, Central and South America. The part played by Portugal in the discovery of Latin America was insignificant when compared with Spain's colonial activity.

For this reason the story of the conquest of Latin America is mainly one of the lives of the Spanish discoverers and conquistadores. The conquistadores had two main aims: to find gold and precious metals, and to convert the native Indians to Christianity. The finest of the conquistadores—Cortés, Valdivia, and Balboa—bestride the age, and must be ranked with the greatest names in history.

Critics of the Spanish Conquest have said that the conquistadores cruelly destroyed two great civilisations. There is some truth in this, but the story must be understood against the general background of intolerance and persecution which prevailed in both Europe and America at the time.

At the end of the fifteenth century Spain was striving to achieve internal unity. Two events marked the culmination of this search. In 1469 the kingdoms of Castile and Aragon were united by the marriage of Isabella and Ferdinand. And in 1492 Granada, the last stronghold of the Moors in Spain, was captured. This marked the final phase in the reconquest of Spain from the Moslems.

The voyage of discovery of Columbus in 1492 was an entirely new venture, and a marvellous coincidence with the fall of Granada. It opened up a field for the ambitions of Spaniards who were newly released from their struggles against the Moors.

𝕿enochtitlan.

An Indian record: Cortés meets Moctezuma, 1519

The voyages of Christopher Columbus

Christopher Columbus was the first European to land in the New
World since the days of the Vikings. His four voyages cover the
years 1492–1504. He planned to sail westwards to Asia, which he
believed to be only 4,000 kilometres away, but landed instead in
America on October 12th, 1492, which is still commemorated with a
public holiday in Latin America.

Columbus was born in 1451 and was almost certainly Genoese
in origin. After being wrecked at sea he settled in Portugal in 1476,
where he studied the work of the Portuguese pioneer, Henry the
Navigator. As a result he began to think the world was round. To
prove this he first proposed his voyage westward to John II of
Portugal who refused to sponsor him. He then went to Isabella of
Spain, Henry VII of England, Charles VIII of France, and once

again to John II. These monarchs did not disbelieve his ideas. Columbus was not the first to conceive of a spherical world; it was a well established notion. Their objections were that the plan proposed by Columbus was impracticable and too expensive.

Isabella was approached twice more by Columbus in 1490 and 1491, and only agreed to support him in 1492 after the fall of Granada, when the reconquest of Spain was complete. Columbus was proclaimed Admiral and Viceroy and Governor of all the lands he might find; one tenth of all profits were promised to himself and his heirs, and he was given a letter from the Queen to the Great Khan of the Far East.

On the first voyage he sighted the Bahamas (October 12th, 1492) and explored the coasts of Cuba and Hispaniola. Columbus brought back natives and gold to show Isabella, and left a small settlement of Spaniards behind. A hero's welcome awaited the explorer, who was soon equipped for a second voyage. He returned to Hispaniola, but found his settlement in ruins. Indians, provoked by the cruelties of the settlers, had destroyed it. This second voyage (1493–1496) extended the Spaniards' knowledge of the New World. Yet there was mounting criticism of Columbus' activities.

In the face of growing criticism Columbus returned to the Spanish court to justify his actions, but he had failed to find gold in any great quantity, and his enemies easily undermined his standing with Isabella. His critics were anxious to destroy the Columbus family's rights in the new lands. When he reached Hispaniola on his third voyage in 1498 he was arrested by a newly appointed governor sent to supplant his authority, and was promptly returned to Spain in chains, but on his return Isabella released him. The fourth and final voyage (1502–1504) broke his spirit and health. He was denied permission to land on Hispaniola, and was ship-wrecked off Jamaica. He returned to Spain to die at Valladolid in 1506, after serving the Spanish crown for twenty-three years. During that time he had made the Caribbean Sea a Spanish lake, and opened up limitless possibilities for discovery and conquest. His fate was typical of many of the greatest servants of Spain. He summed up his own fate after his arrest in 1500 as follows:

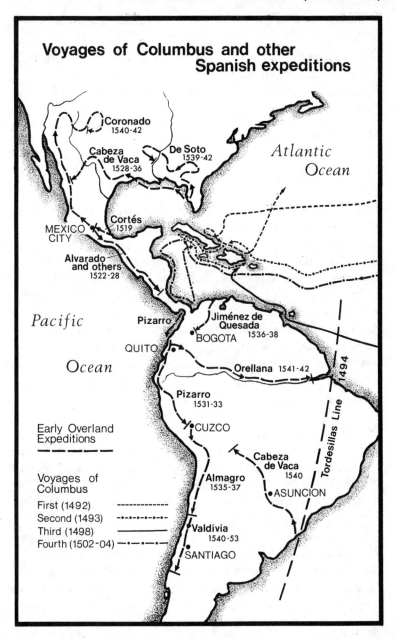

Voyages of Columbus and other Spanish expeditions

Atlantic Ocean

Pacific Ocean

Coronado
1540-42

Cabeza
de Vaca
1528-36

De Soto
1539-42

Cortés
1519

MEXICO
CITY

Alvarado
and others
1522-28

Pizarro

Jiménez de
Quesada
1536-38

BOGOTA

QUITO

Orellana 1541-42

Pizarro
1531-33

CUZCO

Cabeza
de Vaca
1540

Almagro
1535-37

ASUNCION

Valdivia
1540-53

SANTIAGO

Tordesillas Line

1494

Early Overland
Expeditions
– – – – –

Voyages of
Columbus

First (1492)   ------------
Second (1493) -·-·-·-·-·-
Third (1498)   _____
Fourth (1502-04) —·—·—·—

At the time when I was entitled to expect rewards and retirement I was incontinently arrested and sent home loaded with chains.

Columbus remained to his death convinced that Central America was the Malay Peninsula, and that he had reached Asia, and the Spaniards always used the term Las Indias (The Indies) to describe their new Empire.

The conquest of Mexico

Hispaniola was the first centre of Spanish rule in America, and provided a springboard for new conquests. Puerto Rica was conquered in 1508, Cuba in 1511, and Ponce de Leon reached the coast of Florida in 1514. The isthmus of Panama was discovered in 1510 when Nuñez de Balboa set up the first mainland colony in the New World. Three years later he led an expedition across ninety-five kilometres of jungle to the Pacific, and became the first European to set eyes on the great ocean. Balboa, an outstanding leader and most admirable in his loyalty to his companions, suffered the fate of the successful. He was murdered by the orders of Pedrarias, the new governor sent to replace him, while his companions, including the later conqueror of Peru, Francisco Pizarro, took service with the new commander.

Cuba proved to be a better base for the conquest of the mainland, which began in earnest in 1519. Hernán Cortés set out for Mexico in that year, and opened a new phase in the creation of the Spanish Empire. Cortés had come from Spain to Hispaniola in 1504, and settled down as a farmer. He had moved to Cuba with Governor Velazquez, and became a leading citizen in local society. As mayor of Santiago his life seemed moulded into the pattern of a successful 'encomendero' when he was named leader of a new expedition to establish contact with the Aztec Emperor, Moctezuma.

The expedition comprised eleven ships, one hundred sailors, six hundred soldiers, thirteen horses, and seven small cannon. It faced an Empire of twenty-five million, organised into a sophisticated army. The Spaniards' knowledge of the country and the enemy was almost non-existent. Moctezuma, on the other hand, received regular reports of the European movements. Cortés also faced opposition from within his own ranks. Governor Velazquez had deep suspicions of Cortés, and had planted his own agents among the ships to prevent Cortés from acting independently. Cortés and his companions were very capable of treachery and disobedience if they felt they would gain by such action.

Cortés reached the port of Vera Cruz on Good Friday 1519, and proceeded to gain the goodwill of the surrounding provinces. His genius was shown in two events in those first months on Mexican soil. He established a municipality at Vera Cruz which assumed control over all the country, and elected civic officials who in turn nominated Cortés himself as governor and commander of the new lands known as New Spain. Cortés thus freed himself from Velazquez's control, was reconfirmed as leader, and recognised only the Crown's authority. To gain royal support he despatched all the booty so far captured to the King of Spain, Charles I. Cortés also scuttled the fleet which had brought his expedition to New Spain. This prevented any enemies within the ranks returning to Cuba to report to Velazquez, and increased his meagre forces by the addition of one hundred sailors.

In August 1519 Cortés began to move westwards. He capitalised on the unpopularity of the Aztec rulers and formed alliances with native peoples. Those tribes forewarned him of Aztec attacks and augmented his forces. He reached the Valley of Mexico without serious check in October, and on November 9th, 1519, he entered the Aztec stronghold of Tenochtitlán. Moctezuma had decided to trust Cortés who in return seized the Aztec Emperor at the first opportunity and put him in irons. Cortés planned to rule New Spain with Moctezuma as a 'puppet' Emperor. His plan succeeded until the spring of 1520, when the Aztecs rose in rebellion. Cortés who had gone to Vera Cruz to defeat a rival expedition from Cuba, returned to find the Spaniards in a desperate plight. On the islands in Lake Texcoco where Tenochtitlán was situated, they were surrounded by enemies and cut off from the mainland. Cortés saw that the Spaniards had to retreat back to the coast before all of them were killed. On June 30th he led the retreat along the causeways linking the capital with the mainland and fell back towards Vera

Cruz. The 'Night of Sadness', as the day is known, revealed again Cortés' greatness as a commander. He lost two-thirds of his men, all his artillery and small arms, and most of his horses, but he had kept a core of veterans together. Within fourteen months he had regrouped his forces, laid siege to and recaptured Tenochtitlán (August 13th, 1521).

Cortés' military boldness was matched by his wise administration. For three years he welded his conquests into a new empire. His moderation and firmness in this more difficult role showed him to be the greatest of the conquistadores. Those who completed the conquest of Mexico and Central America followed his methods. He gave his lieutenants careful instructions regarding the treatment of native peoples—force was to be used only as a last resort. He rebuilt Tenochtitlán as the capital city and encouraged the Indians to return there. Even after his enemies had undermined his power he continued as a private citizen to foster agriculture and commerce, and to endow churches and monasteries.

Cortés has been denigrated by some as the despoiler of the brilliant Aztec civilisation, but had his policy of conciliation been followed and had he been allowed to carry out the pacification of all New Spain, the excesses of those who followed him may have been avoided. Instead he spent the last twenty years of his life in obscurity, unable to contribute to the establishment of good government. The Conquest of Mexico was followed by the establishment of Spanish rule to the north and south. The Spanish Empire in the sixteenth century stretched far to the north of present day Mexico, into California, as far as the 40° parallel. The great heartland to the east of California was also explored by small groups of conquistadores.

Three expeditions, which are little known, illustrate their heroic nature. Panfilo de Narvaez and Cabeza de Vaca crossed from Florida to Mexico on foot between 1528 and 1536; and Hernando de Soto, who had been with Pizarro in Peru, followed them to his death in 1541. A year earlier Francisco Coronado had explored the south-western quarter of the United States as far as the Mississippi and Kansas Rivers. He was looking for the 'Seven Cities of Cibola', believed to be fabulously rich. He failed to find anything except

Indian villages, but added an area the size of Mexico and four times the size of Spain to the Empire.

Immediately after the successful conquest of Mexico, Guatemala, its southern neighbour, fell to the Spaniards, and Pedro de Alvarado, chief of the lieutenants of Cortés, was made governor. Alvarado's success in pushing south to Panama completed the subjugation of Central America, and all attention could thenceforth be concentrated on South America.

The conquest of Peru

The conquest of Peru matches that of Mexico in terms of audacity, imagination and brilliance. The modest beginnings of this conquest were laid in the 1520s at Panama where Pedrarias still ruled.

A triumvirate consisting of Francisco Pizarro, Diego de Almagro, and a priest, Fernando de Luque, formed a business partnership which operated in a modest way, farming and slaving in Panama. Pizarro and Almagro were socially of a lower standing than Cortés, who had had a university education, for they were illegitimate sons of peasants. Cortés had been thirty-four when he set out for Mexico in 1519, whereas Pizarro and Almagro were both over fifty in 1524. In that year the triumvirate sent an expedition led by Pizarro to explore the Pacific coast south of Panama. In 1526 a joint expedition led by Pizarro and Almagro crossed the Equator for the first time, and contact was made with tribes who knew of the Incas. Almagro returned to Panama for reinforcements, leaving Pizarro encamped on islands lying off the coast of Colombia.

Pizarro's courage and tenacity of purpose were severely tried in his prolonged stay on the islands. At one point a chance to return to Panama arose, and Pizarro drew a line in the sand to test the loyalty of his followers. Those who wished to return to the isthmus were to stand on one side of the line. Those who wished to join him were to stand on the other. Thirteen adventurers followed Pizarro south, including Almagro with the reinforcements. Pizarro succeeded in bringing back more definite news of the Inca civilisation, and he returned to Panama confident and full of hope. He was greeted by the scepticism of the Spaniards in Panama, although he brought with him llamas and gold and silver, and he was thus determined to seek support from the King in Spain. In July, 1529 Pizarro was appointed Governor and Captain General of Peru for life. Almagro, for his part, was only rewarded with the governorship of the small town of Tumbes in north Peru, a situation that angered him, and was to have serious repercussions for the future history of the conquest.

In 1531 Pizarro began the conquest of Peru. He was almost sixty years of age—uneducated but experienced. His expedition consisted of one hundred and eighty men, and twenty-seven horses, and he hoped to conquer a well organised empire of about six million. He was aided, as Cortés had been, by the instability of the Inca Empire itself—the Incas had been divided by civil war which broke out between the sons of Huayna Capac, Atahualpa on the one side, and Huascar on the other.

In November 1532 Pizarro reached Atahualpa's camp at Cajamarca. He invited the Inca to visit him, and at the same time prepared to capture him. He concealed his men around a square where Atahualpa was to be received. The Inca arrived with five thousand men, but these were of no avail in the narrow confines of the carefully chosen meeting place. Spanish small arms fire raked the square, and the horses charged. Atahualpa was taken prisoner and in half an hour the Inca Empire had collapsed. He was offered his freedom if he succeeded in filling a room five metres long, four metres broad and two metres high with gold. This was done, but Pizarro's trickery was not ended. He accused Atahualpa of plotting to do away with his brother, Huascar. A trial followed which was a mockery of justice, and the Inca was summarily executed. The reputation of Pizarro was badly stained by this deed, and he afterwards regretted it. Politically it was a very foolish move because he was now faced with the implacable hostility of the Indians, and besides, many of his compatriots were offended by his lack of honour.

Pizarro pressed forward with his conquest. On November 15th, 1533 Cuzco, the capital city, fell. A Spanish municipality was elected there, and in 1535 the 'City of Kings', Lima, was founded. This new city symbolised the completion of the conquest of Peru, but not the beginning of ordered and settled government.

*Cuzco, Peru, seen from the Inca fortress of Sacsahuaman;
note the grid pattern of Spanish town planning.*

Machu Picchu, Peru, the lost city of the Incas;
a view of the east terraces

Almagro had led an expedition of discovery to Chile, and on his return in 1537 claimed his rights as governor of the southern part of the conquests he and Pizarro had made. A quarrel arose. The two veterans could not agree on their respective claims. Almagro asserted that his share included the old Inca capital of Cuzco. He seized it, captured Hernando, Pizarro's brother, and proceeded to march to Lima, where Pizarro had his headquarters. No agreement with his old comrade was possible, and the two soldiers prepared to face each other in battle. Pizarro first arranged to have Hernando freed, and then met the Almagristas at the Battle of Las Salinas (April 1538). Pizarro captured his erstwhile colleague, had him tried, and then strangled in July 1538. The demise of Almagro did not lead to settled government. The Almagristas led by Diego, Almagro's young mestizo son, swore revenge on Pizarro. They murdered him in 1541, and his bones remain in the cathedral at Lima, encased in glass for all to see.

Diego Almagro the younger was proclaimed Governor, but the royal judge, Vaca de Castro, was sent to take control of the situation. Within a year the Almagristas had been defeated and royal authority was established. The remaining threat to it lay with Francisco Pizarro's other brother, Gonzalo. He lived in sumptuous isolation at Sucre, exploiting the newly discovered riches of the silver mine at Potosí, the present day site of which is shown facing page 64. The threat proved real enough for three years, but ended with Gonzalo's defeat at Sacsahuaman, and his execution in 1548.

Chile and the Río de la Plata

Much of South America remained undiscovered and was conquered only after Peru had been incorporated into the Spanish Empire. Pedro de Valdivia completed the discovery and conquest of Chile begun by Almagro. He was shrewd and practical, and his view of Chile was in direct contrast to that of Almagro. Valdivia recognised the value of farming as well as gold mining, and he found the new land rich and fertile, not a barren disappointment. He followed the Pacific coastline south and founded the cities of Valparaiso and Santiago in 1541. He met determined resistance south of the River

Bío Bío, which was to become the effective frontier between Spanish settlement and the territory of the Araucanian Indians. An epic poem, written by the Spanish courtier, Ercilla, called *La Araucana*, was a fulsome tribute to the fighting qualities of these Indians, who resisted foreign rule until the middle of the last century. *La Araucana* was first printed in Madrid in 1569, and in it Ercilla described the physical and mental attributes of these Indians in the following way:

> They have healthy beardless faces, tall well built bodies with broad shoulders, strong chests and sturdy limbs; they are agile, quick, courageous, lively, valiant, daring, hardworking and impassive in the face of cold, hunger and heat.

When he died in 1554 Valdivia had laid the foundations for successful colonies in southern Latin America, and Santiago had become the centre for exploration across the Andes into present day Argentina.

Expeditions from Santiago east led to the foundations of Mendoza in 1554, and San Juan in 1562. At the same time explorers set out from Upper Peru in a south-easterly direction towards the Plate estuary, founding a line of settlements, notably Tucumán in 1565 and Córdoba in 1573. Sixty years earlier Solís had discovered the Río de la Plata, but there had not been any further expeditions. A settlement had been established at Buenos Aires but it was abandoned to Indians in 1535. The surviving settlers sailed up the River Paraná to Asunción, which remained the only Spanish settlement on the eastern side of the continent until Juan de Garay led some colonists 1,600 kilometres downstream to refound Buenos Aires in 1580. In 1540 Cabeza de Vaca, who had earlier explored North America, crossed the Chaco from Asunción and reached Upper Peru.

By 1580 the Spaniards had extended their Empire to the lines that were to mark its final boundaries. The conquest of Colombia by Jiménez de Quesada, had closed the one remaining gap between Spanish rule in the Caribbean and the conquests of Pizarro to the south. From California to Chile, from the Mississippi to the Río de la Plata, the Spanish controlled a great Empire.

Portuguese America

One vast triangle of land remained untouched. It stretched from Venezuela to the River Plate and from the Atlantic to the Andes and is known now as Brazil. Between the years 1492 and 1580 the most notable feat of discovery by the Spanish in Brazil was that of Francisco de Orellana. Orellana, a lieutenant of the Pizarros, sailed down the Amazon (1541–1542) and returned to the Spanish court full of tales of gold and cinnamon and shapely Amazon women, but when Orellana returned to the area for further exploration he was shipwrecked and drowned.

In contrast to the Spaniards, whose voyages of discovery began with Columbus in 1492, the Portuguese had a tradition of discovery stretching back at least to 1415, when they had captured Ceuta, the Moslem stronghold in North Africa. Their main interest, however, lay in exploring the west coast of Africa, and in 1485 Diaz had rounded the Cape of Good Hope. Portuguese interest in America was non-existent until four Papal bulls were issued by Pope Alexander VI in 1493. The bulls granted the newly discovered lands in the Americas entirely to Spain, but in the following year Spain unknowingly gave up part of her new colonies to Portugal. Under the Treaty of Tordesillas Spain recognised Portuguese claims to lands 20° west of the Cape Verde Islands. (See page 27). Queen Isabella did not realise that by this action she was granting Portugal control of the north east corner of present day Brazil; but King Emmanuel of Portugal recognised his good fortune and got Pope Julius II to endorse the Treaty of Tordesillas in 1506. The Portuguese made no attempt to establish an Empire as the Spaniards did. They had coastal settlements at São Vicente (1532) and at Bahia (1549) but these were in response to fears of French, Dutch and Spanish encroachment rather than colonial settlements in the Spanish sense.

The Portuguese subsequently expanded much further to the west than the Treaty of Tordesillas had laid down, and the Spaniards for their part did not prevent Portuguese America from reaching as far as the foothills of the Andes. This explains why modern Brazil forms such a large part of South America.

Colonial rule in Spanish America and Brazil

The establishment of civil government to replace the rough rule of the conquistadores began as soon as the new areas were subjugated. Who were the new masters of the Indian population? The North American historian, Professor Gibson, identifies three conflicting elements struggling for control in the New Empire. The first were the settlers who held Indians in 'encomienda': colonists were given Indian families to work and carry out services for them. In return the colonists had to provide a Christian upbringing for them and give military service to the colonial government should it be necessary. The second was the Roman Catholic church, which was dedicated to convert Indians to Christianity, to prevent exploitation of them by the encomenderos, and to establish a Christian society. And the third was the Spanish Crown, which was faced with the problem of reconciling the conflicting aims of encomendero and cleric, and at the same time maintaining its own authority over a new Empire.

The Indians and the encomenderos

The first Spanish monarchs of the colonial period in the New World were Isabella (1474-1504) and Ferdinand (1479-1516). They took the view that the Indians were free, and their grandson, Charles I (1516-1556), followed suit. But the Crown also accepted that the Indians could be assigned to settlers for stated purposes. They were not to be bought or sold as slaves, but in practice, from the earliest days of Columbus onwards, laws to protect Indians were abused. The first encomenderos were the conquerors of the Empire. Cortés was such a person, reputedly the richest man in Mexico; but later they came direct from Spain as settlers. These migrants faced continual efforts by the Crown to undermine their position. The most important attempt to achieve this was contained in the legislation known as the New Laws (1542-1543). Under these Indian enslavement was forbidden, new encomiendas were not to be granted, and existing ones were to lapse on the death of the holder. The most important influence leading to the passing of these laws was the work of the Dominican friar Bartolomé de Las Casas known as the 'Apostle of the Indies'. Las Casas spent thirteen years in Hispaniola (1502-1515) as both a priest and an encomendero and became convinced that the encomienda system was evil. He campaigned and wrote continually on the subject. His work, called *A very Brief Account of the Destruction of the Indies*, blamed the colonists for the disappearance of the Indian population and it helped to convince Charles I of the need for the New Laws. Las Casas himself attempted to put his ideas into practice, to persuade Indians to become Christian and accept Spanish rule.

The reality of the situation was very different. The New Laws provoked the rich encomendero, Gonzalo Pizarro, to rebellion in Peru, and led to unrest in Mexico. The laws were amended and Las Casas' experiments in Central America ended in failure. The Crown was forced to adopt more subtle tactics to gain its ends. It began to pass laws concerned with encomenderos reducing their revenues and importance.

The most important factor in the decline of the encomienda was not the encroachment of the Crown but the decrease in the Indian population in the Americas. In Mexico it fell from twenty-five million in 1519 to about one million by 1605. Indians were extinct in the West Indies by the 1540s while in South America decline in population followed a similar pattern to that of Mexico. Diseases such as typhoid, smallpox and measles was introduced by the Spaniard, and was largely responsible for this decline in population. Despite the blastings of Las Casas the encomenderos' treatment of the native people played a minor part in the decimation of millions.

The encomienda had declined significantly within fifty years of the conquest and most settlers had already adopted other methods of making a living.

The Church

The clergy's prestige and its position did not decline so rapidly as that of the encomenderos during the colonial period. The Church began as a powerful moral force in alliance with the Crown, attacking the rapacious encomenderos, and converting the Indians.

It succeeded in both these tasks to a remarkable degree. We have already seen how the Dominican friar, Las Casas, had a great influence on the decision of Charles I to formulate the New Laws. The Church wanted to preserve its position and never attempted to challenge royal authority in the way the encomenderos had. Church leaders were given administrative positions and by the end of the Spanish colonial period the Church had become a force to be reckoned with in every aspect of government. It was the leading landholder in the colonies. It invested extensively in estates, in mines and in buildings. It provided a spectacle of ostentation and splendour in an Empire where most people lived in abject poverty. It has been estimated that Mexico City had over eight thousand clerics, out of a total white population of sixty thousand, at the end of the eighteenth century.

In the sixteenth century the Church was an impressive moral force. The friars accompanied the conquistadores. They had been brought up in the atmosphere of a newly independent Spain, in which religious purity and a sense of Christian duty were pre-eminent ideals. They saw the New World as an area where pagan people could be converted into civilised, devout Christians; and they introduced millions of Indians to Christianity.

But as the frontiers were established and the Empire became a settled area, the friars lost their pre-eminent position in the Church. It was the parish priests who now took over the task of ministering to the converted. Only on the northern frontiers of Mexico and in the area of the Río de la Plata did the friars, reinforced by the Jesuits, maintain their authority. Both friar and parish priest were beginning to be affected by the growth of the Inquisition's power.

This body had been set up in Mexico, Lima and Cartagena in the 1570s to eliminate heresy and unorthodoxy. It aimed to establish pure Christian worship and it jealously guarded the supreme authority it had over the other branches of the Church, brooking no rivals. Nevertheless its powers in Spanish America were limited compared with the authority it exercised in Spain. It tried, without success, to prevent the spread of the ideas of the eighteenth century Enlightenment to Spanish America. Its control did not extend to the frontier areas which were the scenes of missionary activities in the seventeenth and eighteenth centuries; and it had no authority over the Indians because they were considered to be like children whom it would be unjust to subject to the same laws as the white people.

The Jesuits in Paraguay

The missionaries were allowed a free rein on the frontiers. In South America, where the boundaries of present day Argentina, Paraguay and Brazil meet, the Jesuits established their famous missions. The Jesuit fathers governed these missions as separate states, following among other sources the ideas set out in Sir Thomas More's *Utopia*. They regulated the lives of the Guaraní Indians, laid down schedules of work and rest, and time for prayer and worship. They controlled internal movement, and prepared external defences against slave raiders from Brazil. The Jesuits first arrived in 1610 to establish the missions. They had then been forced to move their settlements down the Paraná river to avoid slavers, and finally established themselves in the wedge of land between the Rivers Tebicuary, Paraná and Uruguay. A population of over 100,000 lived for a century in thirty mission settlements of 3,500 people, each one supervised by two Jesuit fathers. Land was cultivated communally, and 'yerba maté', or Paraguayan tea, was exported to provide the missions with essentials they could not produce themselves.

The work of the Jesuits was ended by a royal decree of 1767, which expelled them from the colonies. No other clergy continued their work. The frontier areas in which the Church still maintained its spiritual mission came under royal control at the end of the eighteenth century; hence the process of establishing supreme royal authority, begun with the attack on the powers granted to the first encomenderos, was completed.

The Church for all its material wealth—it held one half of all the usable land in the Empire—made an enormous contribution to the non-material aspects of colonial life. Millions of Indians were introduced to Christianity. The establishment of a Christian civilisation was more rapidly and successfully achieved by Spain than by any other imperial nation. In addition the Church inspired the most notable architecture and art of the colonial period, which emphasised the importance attached to religion. It also developed schools, colleges and twenty universities; and the friars learnt and translated native languages and wrote the stories of the Pre-Columbian civilisations. As a result of their work we have a clearer picture of those ancient peoples.

The Church remains today a powerful force in Latin American society, whereas the legacy of the encomienda is not so evident. But both institutions had to recognise the supremacy of the Crown. The Hapsburgs and the Bourbons, often in spite of themselves, made the power of the Crown all-pervading, for even the Church found Papal bulls were being vetoed, and clergymen appointed behind its back.

The administration of the Empire

The Spanish Crown at first delegated power in order to found an Empire—Columbus, Cortés and Pizarro all enjoyed wide powers. Then it progressively undermined the authority it had granted. The encomenderos lost their independence. The Church, supported by the Crown against rapacious encomenderos, was itself strictly controlled by royal patronage—the right of the kings of Spain to decide the powers of the Holy Church within their realms.

The Spanish idea of Empire involved absolute centralised control by the monarch. Official orders from the king were signed 'Yo el Rey', 'I the King'.

The king ruled his Empire through two main instruments. In Spain the Council of the Indies, founded in 1524, was directly subordinate to the king. It issued laws and dealt with legal cases concerning the colonies. It appointed office holders on behalf of the king.

RAILEMER3ENARIOMO?

son tan brabos y jus ticiero y mal
ptrabaalos y ñs y haze tra uayar co
un palo es les tezrey no en las do
trinas noay re
medio

A friar beats a native Peruvian weaver; contemporary illustration by Guaman Perma

In Central and South America the viceroys were the highest ranking representatives of royal government. They ruled in the king's name. They held authority over everybody and every aspect of colonial life. The viceroys' duties were to maintain civil and military authority, to administer justice, to collect revenues, and to provide for the welfare of the Indians. They had the task of carrying out laws promulgated by the Council of the Indies.

The enforcement of the king's law, however, was not always practicable. Viceroys often did not carry out the letter of the law. For instance, the New Laws of 1542-1543 issued 8,000 kilometres across the Atlantic, proved unenforceable, and the viceroys used the independence of their positions to modify them. Their motto was 'Obedezco pero no cumplo', 'I obey, but I do not fulfil'.

The viceroys were helped by 'audiencias'. These were courts whose members controlled parts of the viceroyalty. They were appointed from Madrid and exercised some authority independently of the viceroys. Members of the audiencias usually served longer than viceroys, and they could rival the authority of a weak viceroy. The Empire was divided into two viceroyalties, the viceroyalty of New Spain, with its capital at Mexico City (1535) and the viceroyalty of Peru with its capital at Lima (1542). Thirteen audiencias were established during the colonial period. Local government within the viceroyalties was controlled by officials, appointed either by viceroys and audiencias or by the Crown. These officials were subordinate to the viceroy and audiencia in which they worked. They ruled through municipal councils or 'cabildos', assemblies monopolised by conquistadores and encomenderos, but these became filled by place seekers. The Crown wanted to crush attempts by former conquistadores to set themselves up as independent, feudal barons. It began to sell public offices to the highest bidder, and even to Spaniards who never came to the colonies: this system of government was designed to maintain royal authority.

The economy of the Empire

The royal officials controlled economic affairs through two separate specialist bodies, the 'Casa de Contratación' and the 'consulado' of

Seville. The Casa de Contratación, or House of Trade, was set up in Seville in 1503. It controlled commerce, shipping and finance with the Indies. The merchants who wished to trade with the Indies had to deal with the colonies through the consulado of Seville, for the consulado, or merchant guild, enjoyed a monopoly of trade with America. It set up branches in various parts of Latin America, especially in Mexico City and Lima, to act as centres for commerce in connection with Seville.

Fleet system

Trade between Spain and the Indies took place in fleets of ships which sailed at regular intervals. Twice a year convoys of fifty ships sailed from the Americas to Spain from special ports. Vera Cruz served Mexico and much of Central America. Portobello on the isthmus of Panama served Peru and most of South America, including Buenos Aires. Cartagena in Colombia served the Southern Caribbean coast. These ports supplied the colonies with European products sent through the monopoly guild of Seville, and they served as the foci for the American products being sent to Spain, especially precious metals, mined in growing amounts after 1550. The convoy system did provide protection for Spanish trade from pirates and interlopers anxious to break the monopoly. Its success in stemming French, English and Dutch encroachments in the second half of the sixteenth century was considerable. Unfortunately the metals which the convoys safely transported to Spain did not enrich the Spanish Crown as much as was expected.

Crown expenditure

Two-fifths of all precious metal received in Spain was automatically taken by the Crown, one-fifth in taxes and one-fifth as a royalty. It is impossible to calculate exactly the total amounts received by the Crown. In the 1540s the Royal Treasury was receiving over two million pesos worth of gold and silver per annum. Between 1530 and 1640 it received at least one million pesos worth per annum. But the Crown spent the money on wars and in defence of Catholicism. Prices in Spain rose rapidly, and the Crown was unable to reduce its expenditure. Charles I borrowed heavily and committed his revenue in advance as debt payments. His son, Philip II, never extricated himself from the situation, and by the time of his death in 1598, Spain's decline had set in.

The flow of easy money from the colonies undermined Spain's industry and agriculture. The monopoly system, by which the colonies would provide raw materials for Spain in exchange for manufactured products, and thus maintain a self supporting Empire, broke down. Spain could not supply the products the colonies wanted. She had established a monopoly system which she could not carry out, and by the end of the eighteenth century the foreigners Spain had sought to exclude directly or indirectly controlled most of the trade with Spanish America.

Bourbon reforms and results

The Crown had established its domination over the Church and conquistadores, but had proved incapable of controlling the system it had set up to govern the Empire. In the eighteenth century the Bourbon monarchs, especially Charles III (1759-1788), made a serious effort to reform and revitalise the Empire.

The Casa de Contratación lost some of its powers. The monopoly of the Seville merchant was transferred to Cadiz in 1717, and then abandoned in 1765, when nine Spanish ports were allowed to trade with Spanish America. Most Spanish American colonies were now allowed to trade with each other, and in 1789 they were all permitted to trade directly with Spain. An attempt was made to bring about genuine reciprocal commerce. Spanish manufactures were exempted from colonial duties, and American goods, such as sugar, cacao, hides and coffee, entered Spain more cheaply than before.

A new system of local government was introduced. A class of officials called intendants was appointed directly by the Crown to the region of the River Plate and Mexico. Two new viceroyalties were created, New Granada (1717) and La Plata (1776), thus undermining those traditional centres of power, Mexico City and Lima. In Spain itself a special Ministry of the Indies was established, and the venerable Council of the Indies lost much of its prestige

Colonial rule in Latin America (1800)

Spanish
1 Viceroyalty of NEW SPAIN
2 Viceroyalty of NEW GRANADA
3 Viceroyalty of PERU
4 Viceroyalty of LA PLATA
Portuguese
5 BRAZIL
Other Powers

and authority. The defences of the frontier areas were refurbished, especially the northern borderlands and the new viceroyalty in the south.

The creaking government of Spain thus made some concessions to her colonists, and the result of the changes was prosperity in some areas, especially La Plata. But taxation remained heavy and the administration still creaked. The reforms came too late and were too limited to bridge the widening gap between colonies and mother country. Forces that were demanding greater freedom for the colonies continued to grow in strength.

Life in colonial Latin America

Colonial society was dominated by whites. The majority were settlers, often called 'creoles'. The minority were temporary officials from Spain, known as 'peninsulares'. The whites represented a wide cross section of Spanish society. The Spanish aristocracy came as colonial administrators. Merchants, farmers, craftsmen came because they imagined they would find prospects better than in Spain. The lower classes could not expect to make fortunes like the peasant Francisco Pizarro had done, but they could reach higher social positions than they would have done at home. The emigrants were Catholic and Spanish, and no encouragement was given to other Europeans who might have wished to settle in Spanish America. In 1550 the whites totalled a mere 100,000 but by 1800 they numbered over 3 million.

The Indians declined rapidly from 40 million at the time of the Conquest to 4 million in the seventeenth century. Those that remained became subservient to the Spaniards. At the end of the colonial period the Indian population had risen to 7·5 million, but most of them were tied to Spanish masters and were subject to debt peonage. Once an Indian had been lent a small sum of money as an advance on wages he could be held to a lifetime of work by a Spaniard, who ensured that the debt was never paid off. This indebtedness was passed on from father to son so that families were held in bondage generation after generation. In this way the Spaniard got round the legal prohibition of Indian slave labour, and still retained a labour supply. The Indian, though in theory protected by law from exploitation, came in practice to live at a subsistence level. He lost his lands to settlers, and as a sign of his status as a second class citizen he was forced to pay tribute. He was held in low esteem by Spaniards, who regarded him as sullen, lazy and shifty. His position in colonial society was wretched.

There were 750,000 negroes in Spanish America in the late eighteenth century. They were imported from Africa to work as slaves, a policy which the Crown encouraged in order to avoid the enslavement of Indians. The conditions under which they lived varied from master to master. Though the negroes were never as numerous or important in Spanish as in Portuguese America, they played a vital part in the economic life of the Caribbean area.

The three races mixed. Spaniards who married Indians were known as 'mestizos', those who married negroes as 'mulatos', and the children of Indians and negroes were called 'zambos'. It is impossible to know how many of each group existed, partly because no accurate censuses were taken, and more especially because the categories were themselves vague. The most specific division of racial groups we can make for this time is as follows: there were 7·5 million Indians, 3 million whites, 750,000 negroes, and 5·5 million people of mixed origin. The total population of 17 million compares with that of 11 million in Spain, and is derived from figures given by the traveller Alexander von Humboldt, writing at the beginning of the nineteenth century.

Agriculture

Life in rural Spanish America was based on two institutions. In the interior, away from the tropical coasts, the hacienda, or landed estate, was everywhere the dominant feature. It produced maize for the Indians, and wheat for the Europeans. It exported hides for leather manufacture in Spain, and on its ranges the Spanish American cowboy developed his distinctive way of life.

In the Caribbean area and on the tropical Pacific coast the characteristic institution was the plantation. Negroes provided the labour force, just as Indians worked on the hacienda. There was a growing trade in sugar, tobacco, and cacao in the eighteenth century, which the plantations fostered.

Mining

Agriculture, however, was not the compelling reason for Spanish interest in the New World. The Spaniards were attracted by the lure of precious metals. Mining became the most important economic enterprise in the Empire. The settlers ignored many other valuable metals in their search for gold, which was found in great quantities, but it was silver that provided the bulk of the precious metals shipped to Spain. The discovery of a mountain of silver in Potosí in 1545 was the prelude to the greatest silver rush ever known. Situated 4,000 metres high, on the barren Bolivian altiplano, Potosí would never have been inhabited but for its silver. An artificial city developed which was said to have had a population of 160,000 in 1650. It was completely dependent on the lowlands for food supplies, which reached it on old Inca roads from the north of the present-day Argentina. The fame of Potosí spread over the world. Called the New Toledo, it boasted thirty-two churches and the most important public building in the Americas, the royal mint. It attracted Spaniards and foreigners alike to marvel at its glories, and the visitor to Potosí today is still surrounded by the beauties of Imperial Spain which survive in this inhospitable setting.

Potosí alone produced £250 million worth of silver, and once the silver boom had ended in the viceroyalty of Peru, it began in Mexico, towards the end of the seventeenth century. The Crown controlled the mines but granted liberal concessions to mineowners, provided it received its due of the 'quinto', a fifth part of all precious metals mined, and all taxes. It maintained a monopoly on the sale of mercury, which was an essential ingredient in the process of separating the silver ore from the rock.

The mining towns were makeshift, lawless centres, where only a few people made the fortunes which everyone who went there dreamed of. The places were only temporary settlements which rose and fell in a few years. Potosí was an exception because for a hundred years it enjoyed a fabulous wealth. Yet even Potosí's decline was rapid after 1650. In 1800 she had only 8,000 inhabitants.

Cities

The Spaniards were urban dwellers, and the hub of colonial society was the city. Among the first acts of the conquistadores was the establishment of municipalities, because they believed that colonial life would not begin unless first formalised through municipal authority. Thus Cortés founded Vera Cruz in 1519, and Pizarro established a new Spanish city adjacent to that of the Incas at Cuzco in 1533. The greatest Spanish American cities were those of Mexico City, founded in 1521, and Lima in 1535. They were the centres of the two viceroyalties and controlled the New World for two hundred years. Mexico City, founded along side the ancient Aztec city of Tenochtitlán, was the leading city of the western hemisphere, at a time when New York was insignificant.

The Spanish city in the Americas was built on the gridiron plan —a network of rectilinear streets and rectangular blocks. The central plaza, or square, was the focal point, and situated around it were the main church, the residences of government officials, government offices, and the main Spanish-owned businesses.

The streets nearest the plaza would house the wealthiest and socially most important members of the white aristocracy. Further away from the centre would be streets devoted to particular trades, for example a street of carpenters and a street of leather workers. On the very edge of the city, areas would be set aside for Indians and the poorer classes. This pattern still survives in the major cities in Latin America to this day.

Class structure

Spanish colonial society preserved strict class distinction. There was a wide gap between the aristocratic few and the Indian/mestizo majority living at subsistence level. A middle class, which might have been expected to develop in the urban areas, did not because industry was closely controlled by the Spanish government, and until late in the eighteenth century there was economic stagnation throughout the Empire. Industry, like agriculture and mining, depended on the exploitation of Indians, negroes, and half-castes. The conditions of work in the largest industries, such as those making textiles and cigars, were appalling. Otherwise, manufacturing was closely controlled by restrictive guilds which prevented competition and tried to reserve their membership to whites.

If colonial society meant white society, there were, nevertheless, divisions within the ranks of the 3 million whites. The creoles resented the dominant position that the Spanish born peninsulares held. The peninsulares monopolised public offices, and controlled leading positions in the Church. They made little attempt to understand the problems of the colonies, and regarded the creoles as inferiors. The latter had some economic power, for they were landowners, mine owners and merchants, and they wanted political power to match it. Charles III's administrative reforms did nothing to break down the growing feeling of hostility between the two groups at a time when goodwill was necessary to preserve peace within the Empire.

Portuguese America

The Portuguese did not finally establish control over Brazil until 1661. The Treaty of Tordesillas in 1494 had involved Portugal in the colonisation of America. According to the Treaty, her legal claim was limited to a thin strip of coast from Para in the north, to Santos in the south, about 1,200 kilometres from east to west at its widest. Portugal's establishment of settlements at Pernambuco in 1530, and São Vicente in 1532, marked her first real interest in the newly acquired land. It was followed in 1533 by the appointment of twelve captains, or 'donatorios'. The donatorios were given wide powers to rule strips of coast extending inland as far as the line of the Treaty of Tordesillas.

This first attempt to establish a form of administration failed because the donatorios were too weak to prevent French incursions. In 1549 John III appointed a Captain General, Tomé de Souza, with strong powers over the donatorios. He ruled as viceroy for four years until 1553. De Souza brought with him to Brazil six

Jesuit fathers who began the conversion of the Indians, and established a strong Jesuit influence on the development of the colony. The most notable of the early captain generals was Mem de Sa, who vigorously supported the Jesuits in their efforts. By 1580 Brazil boasted twenty thousand settlers, eight well-established donatorios, and a lively export trade in Brazilwood and sugar. She also had a few thousand negro slaves.

Foreign involvement (1580-1661)

Between 1580 and 1640 Portugal was under Spanish control. During those years Portuguese settlers began to push westwards into what was legally Spanish territory. The treaty line of 1494 became a dead letter. While this situation was to the advantage of the Portuguese, the fact that Spain's enemies now became Portugal's and began to look with jealousy on Brazil, was not. The earliest competitors for the control of Brazil had been the French. After 1560 Portugal's chief rival was Holland. In the early seventeenth century the Dutch monopolised the world's carrying trade, and through it they had built up close links with the Portuguese trade with Brazil. In 1605 the Spanish authorities prohibited this, and war broke out between the two countries. The Dutch attacked Bahia, the capital of Brazil. They set up the Dutch West India Company, a trading company like the British East India Company, which aimed to oust the Portuguese from Brazil. War between the Dutch and the Portuguese followed in 1625 and lasted until 1661, when the Dutch renounced all claims to Brazil.

The Dutch had established a colony at Pernambuco during the war, and renamed it Mauritsstad after its governor, Prince Maurice of Nassau. They left their unmistakable influence on the towns of north-east Brazil, which is still visible in the buildings there. They improved the sugar industry and methods of agriculture. The most significant influence of the Dutch occupation from 1630 to 1654 on the colonies was, however, a determination to rule themselves. The Brazilians resented their new Dutch masters, and began a long struggle to oust them. Victory was achieved in 1654 with little help from Portugal, and was the first demonstration of Brazilian nationalism. The colonists were impelled to revolt because the supply of negro slaves to Brazil from Portuguese Africa had ended with the capture of Angola and São Tomé by the Dutch in 1641. The settlers were thus deprived of their labour supply which would have spelt disaster for the plantations of the north-east.

The struggle for control of Brazil was being settled, while three racial elements, the Portuguese, Indian and negro, created a society in which the intermingling of the groups was freely accepted. No conscious sense of superiority (which the Spaniard felt) over the Indian or negro existed. The offspring of sexual relations between races were accepted without stigma, and the mixed peoples that resulted played a vital role in the development of Brazil.

Expanding the frontier

By 1661 Brazil had already stretched far beyond the confines of the Treaty of Tordesillas. Settlers explored the Rivers Amazon, São Francisco, and the tributaries that drained to the Plate estuary. Portuguese colonists who settled in São Paulo at the end of the sixteenth century took Indian women as concubines, and their children, called mamelucos, opened up the frontier areas bordering on Spanish America. They raided the Spanish missions on the Paraná for slaves, and opened up lands rich with gold and diamonds. By 1800 Portuguese claims stretched to the footholds of the Andes, 3,200 kilometres further than was originally intended. In the south the Portuguese established a trading post in 1680 at Colonia do Sacramento on the estuary of the Río de la Plata—a favourable position from which to dominate and control the contraband trade flowing into southern Spanish America, and a useful point from which to build up trade links with Potosí.

Economy

The economy of Brazil depended on slaves. In 1800 there were 2 million negroes in Brazil out of a population of 4 million. These negroes worked on the plantations and in the mines. The colony's fortunes rested successively on three main products—sugar, gold, and cotton. Sugar was introduced in 1552 and by 1600 Brazil led the world in production. The Dutch expanded the growing of the crop, but Portuguese incompetence, allied with Caribbean competition, undermined Brazil's monopoly. Gold replaced sugar as the chief source of wealth after 1693. Fevered activity followed as the hinterland of Río de Janeiro, called Minas Gerais (General Mines), was flooded with speculators. Boom towns like Ouro Preto mushroomed to a population of one hundred thousand in the eighteenth century. Diamonds were also found in 1728, and the discovery maintained the mining boom into the second half of the century. The town of Diamantina is a reminder of those days. The mining boom led to the rise of Río de Janeiro at the expense of the north eastern town of Bahia.

Pombal's reforms and their effects

Brazil's trade enriched Portugal's closest ally, Britain, more than the mother country. Portugal was not able to keep even as limited a share of her trade monopoly with Brazil as Spain had done with her Empire. The dictator of Portugal, Pombal (1751–1777), did attempt to revitalise both his native land and the colony, just as his contemporary Charles III was doing in Spain. He transferred Brazil's capital to Río de Janeiro from Bahia, thus recognising the growing importance of the southern part. He encouraged Portuguese trading companies in order to rival British traders and recover a share in Brazil's trade.

The Church

Like Charles III, Pombal also attacked the Jesuits, expelling them in 1759 from all Portuguese lands. His attack on the Church was mistaken, for it played a larger and more beneficial role in Brazilian society, than in Spanish America. The Church had always had a freer rein in Brazil and royal control over its authority was less complete than that over the Church and Spanish America.

The story of the Brazilian Church in colonial times is dominated by the part played in it by the Jesuits. The fathers faced the hostility of the governors, planters, and slave traders in their defence of the Indians, and had little support from the Portuguese Crown. They had provided the few educational facilities available in Brazil, and had not been as opposed to change as their Spanish counterparts had. Pombal's action in expelling the Jesuits marked the influence of the Enlightenment and the prevailing anti-clericalism of eighteenth century Europe, but he deprived himself of potential allies in his programme of reform, and it did not succeed.

Colonial Brazil and Spanish America

Colonial society in Brazil was not a pale imitation of Spanish America. It had distinctive qualities which contrasted with those of her neighbouring countries.

The plantation or 'fazenda', dominated Brazilian life, whereas urban splendour was most characteristic of Spanish America. Sugar exports doubled those of all other products, including gold, from Brazil, while Spanish America was preoccupied with mining and exporting gold and silver. Spanish America was a racially-minded Empire; while Brazil accepted all differences of birth with tolerance. Spanish America, moreover, was dominated by a white aristocracy, especially the peninsulares appointed from Madrid, while little notice was ever taken of officials from Lisbon in colonial Brazil. This contrast between the two Empires seems to stem from differences in the mother countries. Spain, in the years when it impressed its ideas upon the New World, was conscious of its own recent past during which religious uniformity and national unity had been achieved. Portugal had freed itself earlier than Spain from Moorish domination, yet at the same time had absorbed something from the North Africans before it became involved in the New World. Her slow awakening to the very existence of Brazil, and her easy-going tolerance, which is typified by the assimilation of negro and Indian into the Brazilian society, were in marked contrast to Spain's attitude to her Empire. The Spaniards built a spectacular Empire in which a preoccupation with legal forms and rigid distinctions was ever-present. It is not surprising that the coming of independence in Spanish America was violent, long and dramatic, while in Brazil it was achieved quickly and without bloodshed.

The emancipation of Latin America

Latin America freed itself from colonial rule in a space of twenty years, though the actual fighting lasted sixteen years (1810-1826). Portugal lost Brazil, France lost Haiti, and Spain every possession except Cuba and Puerto Rico. Apart from four small colonies that England, France and Holland still held on the mainland of Latin America, only the Caribbean islands remained in European hands. Two colonial empires were toppled unceremoniously, without any official foreign support, after three centuries of rule. The achievement was more remarkable than that of the thirteen North American colonies in throwing off British rule thirty years earlier.

The Wars of Emancipation were the result of a variety of causes. In Spanish America, government remained corrupt and authoritarian. The piecemeal reforms of the Bourbon kings had only served to create greater demands for fundamental reform and the commercial prosperity which came about in Buenos Aires and Havana after the relaxing of the monopoly system only seemed to justify these demands. The creoles, who had previously been excluded from any substantial participation in colonial life, developed an American identity as a result of Charles III's policy. They were influenced by events in North America where thirteen small colonies had overthrown a great naval power, Britain.

Though the grievances of the creoles were real enough, their first actions were directed, not in opposition to the Spanish monarchy, but in support of it.

The effect of Napoleon's invasion of Spain

On March 19th, 1808, Charles IV, King of Spain and the Indies, abdicated his throne in favour of his son, Ferdinand VII. In May both father and son were forced to renounce their right to the throne by Napoleon Bonaparte, and on June 6th a Napoleonic decree proclaimed the Emperor of France's brother, Joseph, King of Spain and the Indies.

Resistance to the decree in Spain was organised by local 'juntas', or committees, which led by the junta at Seville, declared war on the French. In Spanish America a similar reaction to the French domination followed, but the creoles made it clear that they did not acknowledge the overall authority of the Seville junta. The creoles acted patriotically. They were very willing to obey the orders of the Crown, but of no other body. Since Ferdinand was in captivity, legal government had ceased to exist, and the creoles believed that they had just as much right as peninsulares or a junta in Spain, to set up their own provisional government in the name of the King.

Creole risings

The creoles had, in fact, shown their mettle and demonstrated their support for Ferdinand even before Napoleon's actions. When in 1806 the British had made a sudden invasion of the Río de la Plata, the Spanish viceroy in Buenos Aires had fled into the interior, but the creole militia had stood firm and forced the invaders to surrender. A further British invasion in 1807 had resulted in another victory for the creoles, and the authority of Spain was only reimposed by making the local leader a temporary viceroy.

In May 1809, after the installation of Napoleon's brother as King of Spain and the Indies, the creoles seized power in La Paz, and in August there was a minor revolution in Quito. These early seizures of power failed, but in 1810 the creoles were not to be suppressed. A succession of revolutions took place; in April at Caracas, in May at Buenos Aires, in July at Bogotá, and in Santiago de Chile in September. They protested their loyalty to Ferdinand VII, demanding only control of government and trade.

The Seville junta, meanwhile, had resolved in the face of Napoleon's men to summon a cortes, or parliament, to which representatives of both the mother country and her colonies were to be sent. The cortes met in 1812, but it would neither offer the creoles equal status at its meetings, nor freedom to trade with the outside world. This destroyed any chance of avoiding armed conflict between the creoles and the peninsulares.

The Wars of Emancipation

The Wars of Emancipation were fought all over Spanish America, with the exception of a few countries, for instance Paraguay. The creoles fought the Spaniards, and Indians, negroes and half-castes were either spectators or unwilling soldiers. The Wars can thus be described as civil wars, and they were to have a devastating effect upon the prosperous economic life of the colonies.

The first stage of the wars was marked by revolutionary movements which temporarily seized control and were then suppressed by the Spanish authorities. Only in the viceroyalty of the Río de la Plata was the early movement successful.

The Río de la Plata

On May 25th, 1810, the creoles seized control in Buenos Aires and overthrew the Spanish viceroy. They tried to extend the rebellion to three neighbouring areas, Paraguay, the Banda Oriental, and Upper Peru. They succeeded in spreading the rebellion, but not the authority of Buenos Aires. The Paraguayans defeated the expeditionary force sent north from Buenos Aires, and proclaimed their own independence, first from Spain in 1811, and then from Buenos Aires in 1813. In the following year José Rodriguez de Francia was declared dictator of the new state.

In the Banda Oriental, an area of dispute between Portugal and Spain for three centuries, a rebellion led by José Artigas successfully raised the countryside against the Spanish rule. Supported by his cowboy followers, the 'gauchos', he soon threatened to take the port of Montevideo, the one remaining outpost of Spanish rule. Artigas was no longer interested in seeing the native inhabitants of Buenos Aires, the 'porteños', seize control of his land, and war broke out between the two groups of revolutionaries. The resulting unstable situation between 1814 and 1816 was exploited by a fourth interested party, the Portuguese, who saw an opportunity to renew their claim to the area. In 1816 the Portuguese took control of the Banda Oriental, and renamed it the Cisplatine state. The third porteño expedition to raise the standard of revolt in Upper Peru failed, and that country remained, like Peru, a bulwark of royal authority until 1824.

The government in Buenos Aires was itself faced with opposition from the interior provinces. Its authority was resented and its leadership challenged by local landowners. They wanted to establish a federal system of government which would allow more self government in each province of the old viceroyalty and less control from Buenos Aires. In 1816 the Congress of Tucumán declared the independence of the viceroyalty of the Río de la Plata, renaming the independent state the United Provinces, but these constitutional problems remained unresolved.

Chile and Mexico

The other early rebellions in Spanish America were extinguished. In Chile internal rivalries between the two creole leaders, José Carrera and Bernado O'Higgins, enabled the viceroy of Peru to re-establish his authority.

In Mexico two priests led the early attempts at revolution. In 1810 Father Hidalgo raised a motley army of fellow creoles, Indians and mestizos, and marched to Mexico City. He was defeated in January 1811, and his revolt collapsed after his capture and execution in July 1811.

One of Hidalgo's lieutenants, Morelos, a mestizo, revived the rebellion. He successfully convened a congress and an independent government granted his demands when it met in Chiltandingo, and he became the effective ruler of much of southern Mexico between 1812 and 1815. But the two Mexican revolts failed to gain substantial creole support, largely because the strong non-white following that they enjoyed frightened the creoles. The creoles had not envisaged revolutionary changes in the status and position of the non-white classes of society, but merely a transfer of power from the peninsulares to themselves.

New Granada

The other area where Spanish authority was temporarily shaken was the viceroyalty of New Granada. The viceroyalty consisted of the present-day countries of Venezuela, Colombia, Ecuador and Panama. It was in Venezuela that most of the early attempts at rebellion took place.

Venezuela

The precursor of independence in Venezuela was Francisco de Miranda. For two decades before 1810 he had plotted, schemed and sought the aid of foreign governments to overthrow Spanish rule in his country. He had finally persuaded the English government to send an expedition in 1808, to liberate northern Spanish America, when the news of Napoleon's seizure of the throne of Spain reached England. Peace was speedily made between the juntas of resistance in Spain, and the English government on July 4th, and the project for which Miranda had worked was abandoned. But, with or without foreign aid, the creoles were prepared to act. In April 1810 they deposed the Spanish officials, though they had previously claimed to be acting in support of Ferdinand VII. Miranda returned from exile to lead the movement, and in July 1811 proclaimed the independence of Venezuela. He lacked the courage to resist the Spanish counter-offensive, and the rebellion collapsed in 1812, Miranda falling into Spanish hands.

The failure of the rebellion was partly accounted for by Miranda's indecisiveness, but an earthquake on Holy Thursday, April 1812, which wrecked rebel-held territory, but spared that of the royalists, was interpreted as a sign of God's displeasure at the creole rebellion. The most significant result of the first Venezuelan Republic (1811–1812) was the emergence of the creole leader, Simón Bolívar, the greatest figure of the emancipation movement.

In 1813 Bolívar led a second creole invasion of Venezuela and a second Venezuelan Republic was established in Caracas (1813–1814). In September he was ejected a second time from his homeland, and fled to Colombia to organise further resistance. But his attempts were to no avail. In April 1815 ten thousand

Simón Bolívar,
1783–1830,
the Liberator;
detail from painting by
José Gil

José de San Martín,
1778–1850,
the Protector;
detail from painting by
José Gil

Spanish veterans of the Peninsular War landed in Venezuela, quickly crossed into Colombia and put down the independence movement. Bolívar escaped capture and fled to Jamaica in order to plan his next move.

Colombia

While in Ecuador there was no further rising after the failure of the 1809 movement in Quito, in Colombia the creoles did overthrow Spanish rule in 1810. But they then wasted precious time while they argued about whether a federal or a centralised system of government should be established. A somewhat unstable independent government survived in Colombia until 1815.

Simón Bolívar

The second stage of the Wars of Emancipation was dominated by two men. Simón Bolívar, known as the Liberator, and José de San Martín, given the title of Protector after the independence of Peru. Bolívar had already proved himself a determined military and political leader, although still only thirty-two years old.

San Martín was thirty-eight years old in 1816, when the second stage of the Wars began. An experienced army officer, he had served under Spanish colours in the Peninsular War until 1812, when he offered his services to the independent government of Buenos Aires. In 1814 he had been given the command of the Army of the North, and proceeded to establish a camp at Mendoza on the eastern edge of the Andes to plan a military campaign against royalists held in Chile and Peru.

Bolívar and San Martín began the successful phase of the wars of liberation in unpromising circumstances. Bolívar, exiled in Jamaica, endeavoured to get British help without success, but his own belief in the justice and inevitable triumph of his cause sustained him at this time.

The bonds that united us to Spain have been severed.
A people that loves freedom will in the end be free.
These two sentences appear in a letter he wrote while in Jamaica to an English gentleman.

It was Petión, President of the newly independent state of Haiti, who eventually provided him with the supplies he needed to mount a third expedition to Venezuela. On the last day of 1816 he landed in the Orinoco Basin, where he set up headquarters at Angostura (now called Ciudad Bolívar). He was joined by four thousand European soldiers, some of whom were veterans of the Peninsular War. This foreign legion was to prove invaluable in the campaign ahead. He was also joined by the lawless horsemen of the plains ('llanos') called 'llaneros', led by José Paéz.

Bolívar planned to outflank the Spanish commander, Morillo, by doing the unexpected. He prepared to march across Venezuela and liberate Colombia. In May 1818 a patriot army of three thousand men marched west up the Orinoco Valley and its tributaries for 1,600 kilometres. It reached the foothills of the Andes, and prepared to cross them at Pisba. The Spaniards considered the crossing of the Andes impossible because the pass was at four thousand metres above sea level. Bolívar made the crossing, although many of the troops died of cold, and descended unopposed into Colombia. On August 7th he defeated the Spanish forces at Boyacá and four days later entered the city of Bogotá.

Having liberated Colombia, Bolívar returned to Venezuela to complete his work there. He called a congress at Angostura to settle the political future of the viceroyalty of New Granada. It was decided to set up a union of the countries which now compose the region, and rename it Gran Colombia. Bolívar initiated the idea and was elected the first President of the new state.

San Martín

Between 1816 and 1821 San Martín played a notable part in the struggle for independence. From the United Provinces he led his army across the Andes during January 1817, taking the Royalists in Chile by surprise. He defeated the Royalists at the battle of Chacabuco (February 12th, 1817), and then entered Santiago. The independence of Chile followed within months.

San Martín now prepared to mount a seaborn expedition to Peru. With the aid of a British naval officer, Lord Cochrane, a fleet was made ready, and in 1820 it sailed for Peru. On arrival San Martín, anxious to avoid conflict if possible, settled down to a long siege, waiting patiently for popular opinion to withdraw support from the viceroy of Peru. In July 1821 the Royalists at last evacuated Lima and retreated into the highlands of Upper Peru. San Martín promptly proclaimed the independence of Peru, and assumed supreme authority as Protector.

The meeting at Guayaquil

The Royalists, led by the viceroy, La Serna, now held only the highland areas of Peru. To the north, sandwiched between San Martín's forces in Peru, and Bolívar's in Colombia, they also maintained control of Ecuador. The liberation of Ecuador was relatively simple. Bolívar's lieutenant, Antonio de Sucre, supported by troops of San Martín's army, defeated the Royalists at the Battle of Pichincha on May 24th, 1822, and thus liberated Ecuador.

The two leaders now turned their joint attention to deal with the remaining Royalist forces in Upper Peru. They met to discuss this very question at the port of Guayaquil on July 26th, 1822. This was the first and only meeting of the two men. Bolívar wanted to incorporate Ecuador into Gran Colombia, and had in effect done so. He admired the Protector's energy and resourcefulness, but believed him lacking in imagination. San Martín was suspicious of the Liberator, whom he thought overwhelmingly ambitious and rather superficial. The two men were contrasting personalities, who could never have worked together to complete the liberation of Spanish America. They disagreed about the form of government the new states should have, whether republican or monarchical. Bolívar firmly believed that San Martín had personal ambitions to become king of one of the new states, the very idea of which seemed to him 'alien to the virginal soil of America'. San Martín, for his part, found his position untenable. He was not popular in Peru because of his attempts to reach a peaceful settlement with the viceroy. He had lost many troops and his military position was weak. Had he wanted to, it is doubtful if he could have defeated Bolívar, but in any case he had grown tired of the lies that surrounded his name. He resigned as Protector of Peru, and on July 28th he left Guayaquil. His final words represent his disillusionment with his situation:

> I am tired of being called a tyrant . . . of having people say that I want to be King, Emperor, or even the Devil.

San Martín retired to Europe, to live twenty-eight more years in exile at Boulogne in France.

Emancipation completed

No third person was present when the Protector met the Liberator, and a complete account of the famous meeting has never been published. The result of San Martín's resignation was that Bolívar was left free to develop his ambitious plans for Spanish America. Two more years of fighting, broke the Royalists' resistance. After the battle of Ayacucho, December 9th 1824, the Viceroy of Peru, La Serna, capitulated and agreed to withdraw the twenty-three thousand Spanish troops that remained in Peru. The last Spanish garrisons survived at Callao and on the island of Chiloe until 1826.

Bolívar now stood supreme and at the height of his power. A new state of Bolivia, named in his honour, was created out of the region of Upper Peru, and he was invited to plan a constitution for it. He created a remarkable system of government, which showed how much he now believed in a firm centralist state. In his scheme for the government of Gran Colombia he had been strongly influenced by the British Constitution. He had limited suffrage by property qualifications and checked executive power, making a senate the heart of his plan. In his plan for Bolivia we can see how the events of the intervening years had changed his ideas. He had tasted and enjoyed power, and become convinced of the need for a strong executive. His plan for Bolivia called for a permanent benevolent dictatorship. The leading authority on Bolívar's political thought, Victor Beláunde, has written:

> Bolívar wished to accomplish the miracle of uniting the advantages of all systems, and what he did in reality was to unite all their defects.

A view of the silver mine at Potosí in Bolivia seen from the university

Certainly his schemes were breathtaking in their vision. In January 1826 he planned to erect an American federation under his leadership and England's protection, and a Congress met at Panama to discuss the scheme. As this failed he turned to another idea, a Federation of the Andes, which would join Peru and Bolivia to Gran Colombia. This suggestion was resented by the existing governments, and Bolívar imprudently tried to ride roughshod over their feelings. Such actions doomed the Federation and as it broke up, so too did the first federal state, created by Bolívar, Gran Colombia.

The Liberator was now entering the twilight of his career. He was exhausted by his great efforts, and the last four years of his life were beset by failures and disappointments. His constitutions proved unworkable, his friends plotted against his life, and his favourite lieutenant, Sucre, was first thrown out of Bolivia and then assassinated. Bolívar, becoming increasingly disillusioned, began to question the value of the emancipation movement. He died in December 1830 in exile for the third time in Colombia, having been banished for life from Venezuela by his former comrade in arms, Paéz.

> I believe all lost for ever and the country and my friends submerged in the tempest of calamities.

Independence of Mexico

The struggles for independence in Mexico between 1810 and 1815 had been in marked contrast to those in South America, for they had expressed the dissatisfaction of Indians and mestizos, as much as creoles, with the rule of peninsulares. The rebellion of Morelos had ended in 1815, and no further movement for independence took place until 1820, when the creation of an independent Mexico resulted from a desire on the part of all the whites to prevent change rather than bring it about. In 1820 a group of army officers, ready to sail for the colonies from Cádiz, mutinied. Their mutiny was a reaction to the oppressive rule of Ferdinand VII. They demanded the implementing in Spain of the Liberal Constitution which had been declared by Ferdinand in 1812. The upper classes in Mexico,

The Jesuit mission of San Ignacio, Argentina

fearful that such a constitution might be foisted on them as well, determined to break away from Spain. The independence of Mexico was proclaimed on February 24th, 1822, and a conservative constitution, which preserved the traditional power of the Church and allowed for the establishment of a monarchy, was accepted. A regency was formed under Agustín de Iturbide, which was to govern the country until a king was chosen. Iturbide was a creole officer who had established a reputation by putting down the rebellion of Morelos. He now induced some members of Congress to elect him Emperor. On July 25th, 1822, he was crowned Emperor Agustín I. His reign was shortlived: within eight months he had been deposed, and a republic was set up in 1823.

Central America

The former parts of the Captaincy General of Guatemala, which incorporated most of present day Central America, and had been under the control of the viceroy of New Spain, first declared independence in 1821 and then united with Mexico in 1822. The union was shortlived. In 1823 the five provinces of Guatemala, San Salvador, Nicaragua, Honduras, and Costa Rica formed an independent state, the Confederated United Provinces of Central America. The confederation survived as a unit until 1838, when it dissolved into the five independent states that exist today.

Independence of Brazil

The independence of Brazil in 1822 followed the peaceful transfer of power from King John VI of Portugal to his son, Dom Pedro. The episode was accompanied by neither the slaughter nor bitterness that the wars of independence brought to Spanish America.

In 1807 Prince John had fled from Portugal before Napoleon's advancing armies. He had established his court at Río de Janeiro and proceeded to carry out administrative and economic reforms which increased Brazil's prosperity. He also successfully established Portuguese authority over the Banda Oriental in 1816, and forced Artigas into exile. He had acted in Brazil in his capacity as regent for his insane mother, Maria I, Queen of Portugal, and on her death in 1816 he succeeded in his own right as king. Five years later, in 1821, the cortes in Portugal summoned John to return home, and he left his son Dom Pedro as ruler in Brazil. The cortes of Portugal, like its Spanish counterpart, had learnt nothing from the events of the last decade. It expected Brazil to return to the status of a dependency, after she had enjoyed virtual independence from the motherland and had, at the same time, been favoured by the presence of the royal court for thirteen years.

Dom Pedro was commanded to return to Portugal, but refused. He called a Brazilian assembly in June 1822. Three months later it became clear that the cortes in Portugal would not change its attitude over Brazil. Dom Pedro declared independence, and in October 1822 he was proclaimed the constitutional Emperor of Brazil. Portuguese resistance was quelled, and the transfer of government was complete.

Brazil became a monarchy in contrast to all the former Spanish American colonies—Mexico having become a republic in 1823— and the relative ease of change in Brazil symbolised the differences between the Spanish and Portuguese traditions that had been established in the previous three hundred years.

International recognition of independence

Britain and the United States looked with sympathy on the independence movements and benefited from them: they became the main trading partners of the new republics.

For Britain this simply meant an extension of the considerable commercial interests she had built up in the later colonial period and during the wars. Britain's part in the wars, though unofficial, had been of crucial importance. Private citizens had fought with Bolívar, and his aide-de-camp and secretary was an Irishman called Daniel O'Leary. Lord Cochrane had built up navies for the independent states, and money had poured in to help fight the wars. British citizens had privately invested £20 million, in the new republics by 1825, when speculation reached its height.

The British government officially favoured reconciliation between the colonies and Spain; as the latter's ally from 1808 onwards she could do nothing else. But Viscount Castlereagh, the Foreign Secretary, became convinced of the inevitability of separation. When his successor, George Canning, recognised the new states, he was in fact following the lines along which Castlereagh's policy was evolving. The British Government would even mediate between two of the new states to settle disputed territory, as in the case of the Banda Oriental. In 1829 the rival claims of the United Provinces and Brazil to the area were resolved by creating a new independent buffer state, Uruguay.

Britain appointed the first consuls to the new states in 1823, though recognition can really be dated from 1825 when commercial treaties were negotiated with Mexico, Gran Colombia, and the United Provinces of La Plata.

Two years earlier the President of the United States, James Monroe, made his famous statement which laid down that the newly independent states were 'not to be considered subjects for future colonisation by any European powers'. The United States feared Britain's intentions in the New World. Her own independence had been won at considerable cost, and as recently as 1814 Washington had been burnt by British troops.

The Monroe Doctrine did not give the United States any commercial advantage over Britain in Latin America, for the new republics and the monarchy of Brazil had already decided that the country which could best supply the manufactures and capital they demanded was Britain.

At the same time the European powers, who thought of re-imposing Spain's authority over her lost colonies, had to reckon with the pre-eminent naval power of Britain. After 1824 the possibility of recovery disappeared. European powers recognised the new states; and Spain herself began to do so in 1836, consoling herself with the retention of Cuba and Puerto Rico for another sixty years.

The legacy of the Wars of Emancipation

The Wars of Emancipation gave the creoles power, but everywhere they inherited countries ravaged by war. Bolívar had said that the

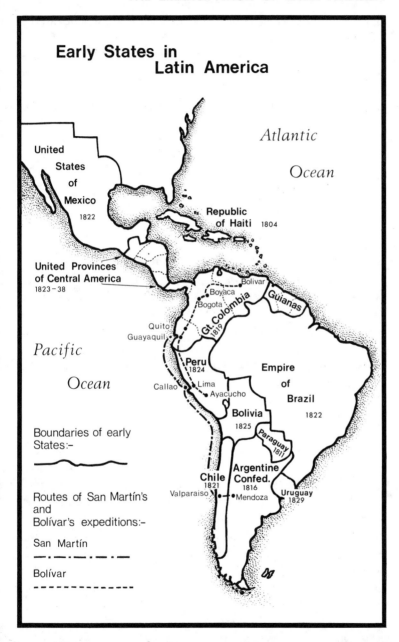

Early States in Latin America

United States of Mexico 1822

Atlantic Ocean

Republic of Haiti 1804

United Provinces of Central America 1823–38

Bolivar
Boyaca
Bogota
Gt. Colombia 1819
Guianas

Quito
Guayaquil

Pacific Ocean

Peru 1824
Callao
Lima
Ayacucho

Empire of Brazil 1822

Bolivia 1825

Paraguay 1811

Boundaries of early States:-

Chile 1821
Valparaiso
Mendoza

Argentine Confed. 1816

Uruguay 1829

Routes of San Martín's and Bolívar's expeditions:-

San Martín

Bolívar

Spanish Americans were unprepared for self-government and this fact became abundantly clear in the years that followed independence. Many of the creoles were impracticable visionaries who formulated unrealistic constitutions for the new states. The problems they faced were legion. They had no experience of government. They had to deal with a mass of people who were illiterate, poor, and scarcely touched by European civilisation. They had to maintain their authority in states which covered many thousands of square kilometres. The under-development of the new states is illustrated by the low population in the United Provinces. The United Provinces of Argentina stretched 3,200 kilometres from north to south, and 1,300 kilometres from the Atlantic to the Andes. It was twenty times the size of England, yet even in 1869, after fifty years of independence, its population was still under 2 million. England's population in 1861 was 20 million.

Most of the new states were in economic ruins, apart from a few coastal ports like Buenos Aires and Valparaiso in Chile, which had prospered. Although investment flowed in, most of it was wasted, and all the states were in debt by 1830. Livestock and crops had been destroyed, the silver mines were derelict with disuse, and labour supplies had been scattered. Venezuela, Bolivia and Uruguay were particularly badly affected, and only Paraguay, by cutting itself off from the outside world, and Brazil, by peaceful change, had escaped completely.

The situation was tailor-made for military rule, and the 'caudillos' or leaders trained by the wars, readily took control. The old creole landowners became the new caudillos. A middle class might have proved a force for stability in this sea of chaos, but such a class would only be found in the towns, and could not be created overnight. The towns were in fact often in direct conflict with the country, which added to the confusion. Buenos Aires was at war with the interior provinces for almost fifty years after the Declaration of Independence. In the United Provinces the lawless gauchos dominated the land. They scorned the settled existence of the porteños in Buenos Aires, and delayed the establishment of effective government for decades.

Chile and Brazil proved to be the exceptions to the unhappy position in which the independent states soon found themselves. In both countries constitutions were adopted which were deliberately conservative, not attempting to grant democratic rights to the majority. In the other new states material progress did take place during periods of stable government, but change could only be brought about by revolution since constitutional processes were non-existent. This explains why Latin America suffered so much from revolution in the nineteenth century, as successive caudillos tried to stamp their personalities on the new states.

The legacy of independence was disorder and disruption, from which few countries escaped, but out of which some, following the lead given by Chile and Brazil, did emerge in the second half of the nineteenth century, and enter a period of material progress. Bolívar had predicted the future very accurately when he quoted Rousseau:

Liberty is a succulent morsel, but difficult to digest.

CHAPTER SIX

The nineteenth century: political and economic change

The independent states gradually escaped from the political instability which the Wars of Emancipation had created. By the end of the nineteenth century most countries had made material progress. Some countries, notably Argentina and Mexico, could in 1900 look back over a quarter of a century of stable effective government, matched by economic growth. These two states joined Brazil and Chile as the leading powers of Latin America. A fifth state, Uruguay, had scarcely achieved political stability by 1900, but had become economically prosperous.

For the other thirteen independent states dictatorships followed each other in bewildering succession throughout the century. Some dictators, like Guzmán Blanco in Venezuela (1870–1888), or Rufino Barrios in Guatemala (1871–1885), were able to control their countries long enough to allow effective economic progress to take place, but the gains were not long standing. The general picture outside the ABC countries (a term used to describe Argentina, Brazil and Chile), Mexico and Uruguay at the end of the century, was still one of political instability and economic backwardness.

Stable government assisted economic progress, and this explains why Brazil and Chile dominated the continent in the first forty years of independence. Once foreign investors had become convinced that other countries were stable, rapid economic progress took place. Let us take a closer look at the development of the four leading powers and Uruguay in the nineteenth century.

The Brazilian Empire (1822–1889)

Dom Pedro raised the cry 'Independence or Death' in September 1822, and was proclaimed the first Emperor one month later.

He imposed a constitution on Brazil in 1824 which lasted for sixty-five years—almost a record in Latin American history—and this helps to explain why Brazil escaped the turmoil of its neighbours. It was in theory a liberal constitution, but in practice the electorate consisted of only a tiny minority of a population totalling about 5 million. A senate was appointed for life, but above all the Emperor held undisputed sway. He could rule virtually unchecked because Article 98 of the constitution allowed him to summon and dissolve parliament, to make all official appointments, and accept or reject all parliament's decisions.

Pedro's constitution was unpopular, and he was personally disliked. His politics at home and abroad were not successful. In 1828 a peace treaty was signed with Argentina, under which Brazil lost control of the Banda Oriental, the Cisplatine state, which she had held since 1816. It became the independent republic of Uruguay. As discontent mounted, Pedro was even faced with riots in his capital, Río de Janeiro. In 1831 he abdicated in favour of his son, and at the age of thirty-three sailed for Europe. He spent his last few years fighting for his daughter Maria's rights to the throne of Portugal. The short, unhappy reign of Dom Pedro I was important for Brazil. He had ensured that the transition from colony to Empire would be smooth, and in addition he had preserved Brazil's unity.

Dom Pedro II (1831-1889)

The new Emperor, Dom Pedro II, was only five years old, and for the next nine years Brazil was ruled by a regency, first of three men, then after 1834 by the single rule of Father Feijo, a liberal priest. The future of Brazil lay in the balance, and the next seventeen years were a critical time for the Empire.

Brazil might have followed all the Spanish American states and become a republic. There was strong support in the north-east for this. She might also have disintegrated into a series of independent states. Both these possibilities were avoided because moderate and conservative opinion rallied behind the boy-emperor. The two political parties disagreed about how the new Empire should be

73

governed, but they were united in support of Dom Pedro II. The Conservatives wanted to retain the 1824 Constitution with its strong central government, and leave the Emperor's personal authority untouched. The Liberals were in favour of a federal structure for Brazil with the power of the Emperor reduced. Neither side could reach a compromise, and in 1840 despairing of agreement, Dom Pedro took the reins of office. He was proclaimed ruler in his own right at the age of fifteen by both parties. Another eight years elapsed before the last rebellions in Rio Grande do Sul and Pernambuco were quelled, but then forty years of unbroken internal peace followed.

Dom Pedro II ruled like an enlightened father figure. He was, despite the constitution, an absolute ruler. Yet he used this personal power for the good of the country, and much of his success in bringing stability to Brazil stemmed from his own identification with the new state. His strong moral attitude to government has been compared to that of Queen Victoria, but perhaps his able management of affairs was more akin to that other long-lived Queen of England, Elizabeth I.

Pedro II's Empire was supported by four influential bodies: the landowning aristocracy, the clergy, the professional classes and the army. The landowning aristocracy, or 'fazendeiros', had been the most important group in colonial Brazil, and their exports of sugar from Pernambuco and cotton from Bahia, provided Brazil's foreign exchange. They ensured that even if the political capital of the Empire was now at Río de Janeiro, its economic heart remained in the north-east.

The clergy strongly supported Dom Pedro II, and relations between Church and state were amicable. In consequence the Church retained its wealth and prestige, and was not subjected to the virulent attacks of anticlerical politicians, which were so commonplace in the Spanish American Republics.

The professional classes had rallied to the support of the boy-emperor in 1831, and they accepted the paternal political system because it provided the stability necessary for trade expansion and increased living standards.

The army also loyally supported the constitution and kept out of politics. The officers showed little inclination to become caudillos, unlike their contemporaries in former Spanish America. In the 1870s these four pillars of the Empire began to lose confidence in the existing system. The fazendeiros found their very existence threatened. They depended on slave labour, but the British government had insisted on the ending of the slave trade as early as 1830. The letter of the law was not followed, and it took another twenty years before the trade was finally eliminated. Slavery, however, still existed. In 1863, following President Lincoln's emancipation act in the United States, Brazil remained the one major western country still allowing slavery. Pressure for abolition mounted. In 1871 a law was passed by a leading Brazilian statesman, Baron Río Branco, freeing the children of slave mothers. In 1872 census figures showed that for the first time there were more free coloured people than slaves. By 1888 the total number of slaves left on the plantations numbered about 750,000, and the end of slavery was in sight.

The Emperor objected to the attempts of the Roman Catholic Church to increase its influence. He particularly resented its attempts to make the priesthood and other religious orders abjure freemasonry—Dom Pedro was himself a freemason. In 1875 he had tried and imprisoned two bishops who had imposed interdicts on lay brotherhoods in which masons were active. The bishops were released, and Dom Pedro's prestige was undermined.

The professional classes became dissatisfied with the status quo. As their importance increased so did their demands for more power. They gave support to a new Republican Party founded in 1870. They pressed for an enlargement of the franchise: even in 1887 the electorate only numbered 250,000 out of a population of almost fourteen million. They were very sympathetic to the new economic influences from Europe, which were forcing changes in the traditional pattern of Brazilian society.

In 1840 Brazil had a population of 6 million, scattered in the old settlements on the coast stretching from Río Grande do Sul in the south as far north as the Amazon delta. The only interior province where any settlement of consequence had developed was in Minas Gerais, following the discovery of gold one hundred and fifty years before. Gilberto Freyre, the Brazilian writer, has said that the majority of Brazilians continued to live in the Middle Ages. The technology of Western Europe's industrial revolution could change the situation.

Coffee growing in the Paraiba Valley between Río de Janeiro and São Paulo developed on a large scale during the 1850s. It attracted labour from the north-east, and a new rural aristocracy evolved. Businessmen and financiers became more important. They used capital from Europe, especially Britain, to develop a railway system, textile factories, banks, the telegraph, and steamship companies. The best known of these financiers was Baron Mauá who had started his business career at the age of nine and later built Brazil's first railway in 1854, introduced the first gas light to Río de Janeiro, and the first steamboat to the Amazon.

A few immigrants from Europe also began to arrive in the 1850s. In the last thirty years of the century the trickle became a flood. Immigration was to increase from an average of twenty thousand a year in the 1870s, to fifty thousand in the 1880s, and to one hundred thousand a year in the 1890s. The total population of Brazil, which was ten million in 1872, had reached seventeen million by 1900.

The loyal supporters of the Empire, the Church, professions, landowners, had been alienated and it was the army, the most loyal of all, which gave the 'coup de grace' to Dom Pedro's rule. The army's disillusionment with civilian rule followed their experience in the one foreign crisis which affected Dom Pedro's reign—the war of the Triple Alliance (1864-70). The war, fought between Paraguay and her three neighbours, Brazil, Argentina and Uruguay, was caused by a complex series of events which date back at least to the 1840s. Two main causes should be mentioned: there were disputes between Paraguay and both Brazil and Argentina over frontier boundaries and the free navigation of rivers; and all three states were involved in the internal politics of Uruguay, where the government, 'Blanco', party looked to Paraguay for support, and the opposition, 'Colorado', party looked to Brazil and Argentina.

A nineteenth century print of Río de Janeiro, capital of Brazil 1763-1960, and below, Brasilia, the present capital of Brazil

The allies won the war and Brazil took the greater part of the spoils. Her army officers had tasted power for the first time, and they returned home inflated by success and determined to exercise more power in Brazil itself. Some army officers seized power there on November 15th, 1889. The next day the newspapers announced that a republic had been established. Dom Pedro abdicated and sailed to exile in Europe.

The sudden collapse of the Empire was deceptive. The Emperor had not realised the significance of the economic changes nor understood that the bases of his Empire had been eroded.

Chile: the Conservative and Liberal Republics

Just as the fazendeiros had ensured that Brazil enjoyed stability during its early decades of independence by supporting Dom Pedro II, so the Chilean landowners, or 'hacendados', established a sensible constitution after independence.

The 1833 constitution gave the President of Chile the power Dom Pedro wielded in Brazil. The first President, Joaquín Prieto (1831–1841), allowed his chief minister, Diego Portales, to control affairs. Portales laid the basis for the stability Chile enjoyed for the next sixty years. He crushed the caudillos. He organised a strong civilian party, the Conservatives, or Pelucones, who monopolised power for thirty years. He won Chile's first war against the combined strength of Peru and Bolivia. Portales' Constitution of 1833 established a highly centralised republic with a two chamber parliament elected by property owners, who numbered fifty thousand in a total population of five hundred thousand. His work was consolidated by two succeeding Presidents, Manuel Bulnes (1841–1851), and Manuel Montt (1851–1861), who encouraged foreign investors and immigrants.

The immigrant numbers never reached those of Brazil, Argentina, or Uruguay, yet their significance was considerable. One hundred thousand immigrants entered Chile in the course of the nineteenth century, and the first arrivals, the Germans, opened up the forest region of Chile to the south of the old Spanish frontier on the River Bío Bío, where the Araucanians still lived unconquered. This area bears strong traces of German culture and language. The foreign investors began to make extraction of the copper in the northern desert and coast at Concepcíon possible. The first railways were built in the 1850s, while the electric telegraph and the steamship linked the young country with Europe and the United States.

President Bulnes established a Chilean presence at the very foot of America in Patagonia, creating the town of Punta Arenas in 1847. He also encouraged educational progress. Chile became the intellectual and cultural leader of Latin America, attracting outstanding Americans like Andrés Bello, who founded the University of Chile, and Domingo Sarmiento, who was the first President of the Teacher Training College in Santiago, and later President of Argentina.

This cultural development was matched by an increasing demand for more political freedom. When Manuel Montt succeeded as President, it was only after the opposition Liberal Party, the Pipiolos, had tried to prevent his election by force. Montt's Presidency was overshadowed by these rumblings of political discontent against the autocracy, and so he made concessions to the Liberals. He passed a law allowing haciendas to be divided up, rather than be passed on intact to the eldest son of the owner. He abolished the right of the Roman Catholic Church to a compulsory tithe. The conservatives lost clerical and landowner support. Montt went further. Faced with criticism from the traditional sectors of Chilean society he agreed that the Liberal choice for the next President, José Pérez, should be accepted. The Liberals, Pérez (1861-1871) and his successor, Federico Errázuriz (1871-1876), accelerated the process of reform. They also reduced presidential powers, while the authority of Congress grew. The decline of the autocratic element in Chilean politics was reflected in the loss of influence of both landowners and clergy. As in Brazil, new economic forces were at work. A rising middle class in Santiago and Valparaiso was making its presence felt, though it would not be able to wrest power from the traditional ruling classes and control affairs for another fifty years. Commercial and business interests steadily grew in importance and influence.

This history of Chile in the last quarter of the nineteenth century was dominated by two significant events. First, the War of the Pacific (1879-1883). Chile had a long standing difference with Bolivia over the boundaries of their respective countries in the Atacama Desert. The rival claims suddenly became important when the large deposits of nitrate found in the region in 1866 became commercially valuable. Its importance as a fertiliser and in the making of explosives was soon realised.

With British capital, Chilean miners began extracting the nitrate in Bolivian held Antofagasta. The Chilean government was anxious to gain as many privileges as possible for its nationals, and pressed the Bolivians to grant them. The Bolivian government, hard pressed by instability at home, could only agree, but at the same time allied itself with Peru in 1873. Peru herself owned nitrate deposits in the province of Tarapacá, north of Antofagasta. Differences between Chile and Bolivia might have still been settled without conflict, for the Bolivian President agreed in 1874 not to increase existing taxes on Chilean enterprises in Antofagasta.

Four years later, however, a new President, Hilaríon Daza reversed the decision. He raised the export taxes which the Antofagasta Nitrate Company had to pay. War followed. Chilean troops occupied Antofagasta in February 1879. The Chilean government demanded the ending of the treaty of alliance between Bolivia and Peru, and when they refused to comply, attacked the latter. The Peruvian fleet was defeated, and Chilean troops occupied Tarapacá. By June 1880 Chileans had also seized two other southern provinces of Peru, Arica and Tacna, and in January 1881, even occupied the capital, Lima. Peru was forced to agree to humiliating peace terms in 1883 under the Treaty of Ancón. She lost Tarapacá and Arica to Chile, and only recovered Tacna in 1929 after half a century of wrangling. Bolivia, for her part, lost her Pacific coast province of Antofagasta, and with it her access to the sea. Bolivia's relations with Chile have never been friendly, and although Chile agreed to and did construct a railway to provide an export route for Bolivia's minerals, it was poor compensation for her lost territory and wounded national honour.

The War of the Pacific confirmed Chile's supremacy over her two northern neighbours. She had gained eight hundred extra kilometres of coastline and over 130,000 square kilometres of new land. The Atacama Desert may have been a forbidding stretch of land but it was to provide the major share of Chile's revenue until the close of World War I. The production of nitrates expanded rapidly after 1883. In the 1890s 60% of government revenue came from nitrates. Other foreign investment increased substantially as well, and the new President of Chile, José Manuel Balmaceda, who succeeded in 1886, was head of a confident, prosperous nation.

The second major event now took place. Balmaceda tried to reverse the balance of political power which existed between the President and Congress. Since 1861 presidential power had declined at the expense of Congress as a result of the reforms of the Liberals (1861-1876). The result of the new President's action was to bring about a clash between the two which has been compared to the struggle between Charles I of England and his parliament, over two centuries earlier.

Balmaceda was determined to carry out a revolutionary programme. It included the nationalisation of foreign enterprises, including nitrate companies. He would not tolerate opposition; Congress, supported by British financial interests, led by the 'Nitrate King', John Thomas North, was equally determined to resist. Balmaceda could, under the 1833 constitution, veto congressional opposition but this right had been abolished in 1885. In 1890 matters reached a climax. Congress refused to pass the President's budget. Balmaceda assumed dictatorial powers, and declared it approved. Congress stood firm. Civil war followed. Congress had the support of the Chilean navy as well as foreign financial interests. As soon as the navy had seized the nitrate ports Balmaceda was deprived of its revenue. In August 1891 he recognised the hopelessness of his situation, resigned and committed suicide.

The effect of Balmaceda's struggle with Congress was to further weaken the presidential power. For the next thirty-three years (1891-1924) one hundred and twenty major cabinets rose and fell. The era of political stability had come to an end.

Argentina (1816-1916)

Chile's orderly progress after independence was in marked contrast to that of her neighbour Argentina. Yet, so successful had the latter been in escaping from civil disorder and the influence of the caudillos after 1861, that by the end of the century she was the leading state in Latin America. The transformation, especially in the last three decades of the nineteenth century, was spectacular. Population more than doubled between 1864 and 1897, from under 2 million to over 4 million, immigration accounting for almost all the increase. British investment rose from £20 million in 1880 to over £200 million in 1900. Seventeen thousand kilometres of railway existed in 1900, where there had been less than eight hundred kilometres thirty years before. These statistics would be remarkable in the development of any country. They are particularly so in the case of Argentina where they followed decades of civil war.

The United Provinces of La Plata, as Argentina was first known, had successfully broken away from Spain in 1816, but in its early years its very existence seemed to be in doubt. Two main problems faced the independent state. First it needed to consolidate its independence. The expeditions to Paraguay and Bolivia, and its involvement with Brazil over the future of the Banda Oriental, illustrated this concern with defence. In each case the United Provinces failed to maintain their claims to the areas. The weakness of the United Provinces also followed its inability to settle a second problem, which was whether the government of the new state was to be centralised, dominated and controlled by the city of Buenos Aires, or federalised, with each province, including the province of Buenos Aires, in control of its own affairs. In the 1820s centralist forces controlled the government but the fall of the President, Bernardino Rivadavia, in 1827 paved the way for the emergence of a provincial caudillo, Juan Manuel Rosas.

Rosas (1829-1852)

Rosas ruled Argentina from 1829 to 1852. He described his country in 1830 as a 'chain of petty republics', and he proceeded to exercise his particular brand of tyranny over his fellow caudillos. Rosas was born in the province of Buenos Aires in 1793. He had developed a reputation as an Indian fighter on the frontier, and had risen in 1829 to be governor of his native province. Each province was ruled by the caudillo who happened to be the strongest local leader. In the United Provinces the caudillo ruled over vast empty plains where the 'gauchos', the mestizo cowboys, and the Indians were the real masters. The gauchos made their own laws with the knife, paying scant attention to directives from the capital, Buenos Aires. Rosas knew the nature of the gauchos and his rule smacked of their violent way of life, but he was strong enough to subdue them.

He came to power as a federalist in opposition to the mighty influence of the city of Buenos Aires, and then proceeded to act like a centralist. During the twenty-three years of his rule Rosas made no effort to solve Argentina's problems of government. While Chile and Uruguay provided oases for intellectuals fleeing Rosas' cultural desert, education was ignored in Argentina. Immigration was discouraged, arable farming lapsed, and commerce outside Buenos Aires stagnated. He ruled with an iron hand, and with the aid of a secret police force. Only in Buenos Aires was there support for the dictator. The porteños reaped the benefit of the monopoly of the commerce they enjoyed, and supported him during the difficult years between 1838 and 1850, when Buenos Aires was blockaded by first a French and then an Anglo-French fleet.

Independent Uruguay, long coveted by Rosas, was the cause of these blockades. Rosas supported one party in Uruguay, but Britain and France were fearful lest he should control both sides of the River Plate by making the Banda Oriental a client state. The caudillos of the interior provinces resented the economic domination of Buenos Aires. In 1851 General Justo Urquiza, Governor of the Province of Entre Rios, rose in revolt. He joined forces with the neighbouring province of Corrientes, and with Brazilian and Uruguayan help raised Rosas' siege of Montevideo in 1851 and met and defeated the dictator himself at the battle of Monte Caseros in 1852. Rosas escaped on board an English ship and added his name to the list of famous Latin Americans who ended their days in the Old World, in his case as a country gentleman in Hampshire.

Rosas has become a romanticised figure, remembered as a defender of Argentina's national sovereignty and honour against foreign aggression. This explains the revival of interest in his rule during the government of President Perón. Rosas' rule seems sterile when set against either Rivadavia's economic policies in the 1820s or the later establishment of prosperity and unity. Domingo Sarmiento, a bitter opponent of Rosas and an exile in Chile during his rule, wrote his classic book *Facundo* as a criticism of all that Rosas appeared to stand for. Sarmiento explained Argentina's trouble in terms of a conflict between Civilisation, represented by urban settlement and economic growth, and Barbarism, represented by the lawless gauchos and caudillos.

Unification (1852-1880)

Urquiza was a caudillo who wanted to see the prosperity of Buenos Aires more widely spread, but he could not solve the dilemma of choosing between federalism and centralism. The capital city refused to accept a new constitution which was agreed at Santa Fe in 1853, and a state of armed neutrality existed between the two parties. In 1859 this developed into open war which continued until the decisive battle of Pavón in 1861. Urquiza lost the battle and the Buenos Aires party was victorious. The porteño leader, Bartolomé Mitre, became the next President of the Republic, and then decided to accept the Santa Fe constitution of 1853. The constitution, which embodied a compromise between federalism and centralism showed the keenness of all Argentinians to settle their differences. Eighteen years later the interior provinces finally accepted the city of Buenos Aires as the federal capital, the city of La Plata becoming the new provincial capital of the province of Buenos Aires in 1880.

Economic transformation

The economic changes which followed the fall of Rosas ushered in an era of unparalleled prosperity. There were two phases of this change. First between 1853 and 1880, while Argentina settled its constitutional disputes, the policies of Rosas were reversed. Urquiza and the first three Presidents of the United Republic,

Mitre (1862-1868), Sarmiento (1868-1874), and Nicolás Avellaneda (1874-1880), all encouraged immigration, foreign investment and modern technology as the bases for developing Argentina. Urquiza built the first railways, beginning with ten kilometres in Buenos Aires, opened in 1857. Mitre added 1,300 kilometres of track during his presidency.

During the years 1868 to 1874 immigration increased by 280,000 and between 1870 and 1880 rose by 750,000. Avellaneda's great service to the nation was in the 'Conquest of the Desert', carried out in 1879 by General Julio Roca. Pampa lands to the south of the province of Buenos Aires were opened up for colonisation. By 1880 the framework for much faster change had been laid: immigration continued to increase; foreign investment rose, which included about £30 million of British capital; and modern technology, in the form of railways, wire fencing to divide up the open pampa, and farm machinery, was introduced. The British played the most important part in this development, providing technical expertise, capital and thousands of sturdy settlers.

This was also a period of progress and education. Mitre and Sarmiento encouraged educational progress, and with the help of Horace Mann, the North American educationalist, set up a public school system, which rivalled that of Chile; indeed Sarmiento became known as 'the schoolmaster President'.

The second phase of the transformation lasted from 1880 to 1914, during which time an economic explosion took place. Population increased from 2,600,000 to 7,885,000, immigrants accounting for over 2 million of that number. Most of the immigrants came from Italy and Spain, and the majority settled in their port of entry, Buenos Aires. The population of the capital increased from 500,000 in 1880 to over 2 million in 1914. British investment reached staggering proportions. In 1914 it totalled £428 million, compared to £30 million in 1880. This vast sum had been used to build railways—there were 32,000 kilometres in use in 1914—meat packaging plants, dock installations, and public utilities. Britain provided Argentina's material benefits and in return received the agricultural wealth of the vast pampa.

Agricultural production responded to the increasing demands of industrial Europe. Argentina provided ideal conditions for a rapid expansion of this sector of the economy: cheap land in abundance, sufficient labour, and railways to transport produce and cattle to the port of Buenos Aires. In 1876 the voyage of the *Frigorifique* had shown the possibilities of taking frozen meat to Europe, and in 1882 the first frozen meat plant, or 'frigorífico', was opened. After 1900 the export of meat became more and more important. In 1905 she had overtaken the United States, not only as the leading supplier to Britain, but also the major exporter of meat in the world. In 1909 she was also the largest exporter of cereals in the world. The completeness of the agricultural revolution can best be understood by remembering that in 1870 Argentina had been an importer of foodstuffs.

As in the years of the first great economic expansion, so also the years between 1880 and 1914 witnessed great educational changes. The rate of literacy had reached 65% in 1914, and Argentina could boast one of the best public schools systems in the world.

In the years 1880–1914 little progress was made towards extending economic prosperity to the majority of Argentina. Rich 'estancieros', or landowners, controlled all aspects of the republic's economic and political life. They bought up all the public land which was freely offered for sale as the frontier moved westwards and south. Land purchases had been carefully controlled in the United States by the Homestead Act of 1863, which limited family purchases to sixty-five hectares, and helped encourage maximum efficiency, but in Argentina there was no control over the size of holdings a man could have, and so a small yeoman farmer class never developed. The average size of holdings was four hundred hectares, and in 1914 over three-quarters of all land was held in farms of one thousand hectares or more.

Resentment of this economic and political monopoly grew, especially in the 1880s, when corrupt government helped to lead to a financial crash in 1890, threatening to make the British financiers, Baring Brothers, and even the Bank of England, bankrupt. A radical party was formed called the Unión Cívica, which pressed for electoral reforms. A Socialist Party led by Juan Justo, and anarchist-syndicalist groups composed of Spanish and Italian immigrants supported his movement, and also demanded other radical changes. The landowners did not know how to react. They had to recognise that the majority of Argentinians had little in common with their traditional ideas. In particular, the immigrant was refused equal status with the native. He had to complete two years' residence to become naturalised, and even then, although he was subject to military service, he did not have the right to vote, nor the right to hold public office. In 1914 only 2·3% of foreign born residents in Buenos Aires had become naturalised.

Argentina's golden years, marked by this phenomenal expansion which has few parallels in world history, covered up real divisions in society between the prospering oligarchy and the urban workers and immigrants. Popular hostility towards foreign, and especially British, control and influence over Argentina increased, and indirectly threatened the predominance of the oligarchy. In 1896 Justo wrote: 'Today our country is tributary to England.' The landowners were in fact to remain Argentina's rulers for another thirty years after the outbreak of World War I in 1914, and Britain continued to be both Argentina's leading importer and exporter for many years. But 1914 certainly marked the beginning of the end of the successful domination of the young republic's life by the estanciero minority.

Mexico (1823-1910)

The transformation of Mexico parallels that of Argentina. Mexico had, in 1900, become one of the four leading states of Latin America, despite half a century of even greater disorder than Argentina experienced after independence.

The era of Antonio de Santa Anna (1824-1855)

The early years of independence were turbulent. The brief flirtation with monarchy under Iturbide was followed by the establishment of republican rule in 1823. A constitution was adopted which was modelled on that of the United States. The federal system thus established divided Mexico into nineteen states, each electing its own governor and legislature. A system of liberal democracy was to be adopted. Both ideas were unrealistic. Spain had ruled the viceroyalty from Mexico City as a centralised state, and there was no tradition of democracy. The constitution was doomed to failure, and in the confusion which followed, the caudillos seized control. No one caudillo emerged like Rosas in the United Provinces to control the others, let alone a conservative leader like Portales or Dom Pedro II, who would rule in an enlightened manner and provide stability. One man's name recurs constantly during the first thirty years of independence, Antonio de Santa Anna, who was President six times. During the years 1824 to 1855 there were forty-six changes of President, and Antonio de Santa Anna always remained either on stage, or in the wings, ready to take control. He behaved like a figure in comic opera, yet exercised great influence on events. In 1833 he allowed the anti-clerical liberals to lauch a comprehensive attack on the power of the Church, while he, the President, remained in the country, pleading ill-health. Within a year he returned to the capital in the van of the Catholics, posing as the 'Saviour of the Church'. Congress was dissolved, anti-religious laws suspended, and Te Deums were sung in praise of Santa Anna.

The liberals with their anti-clericalism, and the conservatives, eager to defend the clergy's power, made certain that one of the dominant issues during the early years of independence would be the question of Church and state relations. Another central issue never satisfactorily settled in the early years was the political problem of centralism versus federalism: underlying Mexican life was incessant anarchy and disorder. Governments were always in debt, and depended on loans. Mines had not recovered from the effects of the Wars of Independence. The mass of Indians was illiterate and uncomprehending. Independence did not bring them improved status any more than it did the mestizos. The liberals did try to change the situation but their attempts at reform were blocked by army officers like Antonio de Santa Anna, who wanted the maintenance of creole and clerical supremacy. Only after a

Benito Juárez,
1806–1872,
reformer
President
of Mexico

foreign war and the loss of half of Mexico's territory could reform make its impact.

In May 1846 war was declared between the United States and Mexico. The cause of the war was ostensibly rival claims to Texas. In the 1820s United States settlers had moved into Texas and begun pressing for secession from Mexico. In March 1836 Santa Anna had crushed a rebellion of settlers at the Alamo, although a month later he was defeated and captured. Texas remained unsubdued, and for all practical purposes independent of Mexico. In 1845 the United States Congress voted to annex Texas, and war followed. The future of Texas was an important issue, but the United States also hoped to get control of California, then under Mexican control. The United States did attempt to settle her claims peacefully, but Mexico refused to see her representative.

In the war that followed the Mexicans were defeated. Texas, California, New Mexico and most of Arizona were ceded to the United States in return for $18 million compensation. Five years later, in 1853, the southern part of the State of Arizona was bought for $10 million on behalf of the United States government by James

Gadsden. Gadsden's purchase completed the expansionist move-ment of the United States in the south-west, which had cost Mexico half its territory, and involved her in the only war between the United States and a Latin American power. It also marked the demise of Santa Anna, who had accepted Gadsden's offer.

Juárez and La Reforma (1855-1876)

The liberals recovered power, and a new reform movement promised a solution which would allow Mexico a chance to escape the cycle of revolution and reaction which had plagued its first thirty years of independence. This movement, La Reforma, was to provide the inspiration for the Mexican Revolution in this century, but its immediate result was to plunge the country into a bloody civil war, which involved foreign powers.

The liberals attacked two institutions, the Church and the landed estates. In November 1855 the law which carries the name 'Ley Juárez' was passed. It suppressed the private law courts of the Church and the army, both of which had enjoyed a privileged position. The author of the law, Benito Juárez, was a pure Zapotec Indian, who had shown great integrity and determination as the Governor of Oaxaca. He became the hero of Mexican nationalism, the symbol of the assault on privilege. Another law (which was named after Juárez's lieutenant Lerdo), the 'Ley Lerdo', aimed to deprive the Church of its land.

The conservative forces rallied to defend the status quo, and opposed the liberal constitution of 1857. Civil war broke out, Juárez and the liberals holding the port of Vera Cruz with its customs revenue, the conservatives occupying Mexico City and the highlands. After three years of fighting Juárez recaptured the capital and the opposition fled. He was faced with an empty treasury, and in July 1861 had no alternative but to suspend payments of external debts.

Britain, France and Spain were all affected by this drastic measure, and resolved to occupy parts of the Mexican coast in order to enforce their payment demands. They disclaimed any intention of territorial gain or special advantage, and Britain and Spain

Manet's painting of the execution of Maximilian

promptly withdrew, once agreement with Juárez had been reached. The French remained, and proceeded to establish the Emperor Napoleon's young relative, Maximilian, as Emperor of Mexico. The outcome was wearily inevitable: civil war broke out again. Maximilian's simple sincerity was a hopeless support against either Juárez, the national hero, or the conservatives who were fighting with him, but who proved fickle in their loyalty. Only military support from the French could preserve Maximilian's throne, and in October 1865 French troops were ordered to leave. In March 1866 the last French troops left Vera Cruz, and in May 1867 the Emperor surrendered. On June 19th, 1867 Maximilian was shot. The French painter Edouard Manet reconstructed this dramatic scene on canvas in his Paris studio a few months later. Juárez was now the undisputed President of Mexico. In the five years of life that remained to him (1867-1872) he provided the most enlightened government that his country had enjoyed since the days of the viceroyalty. On his death his mantle fell on the mestizo Porfírio Díaz who was to adopt a much more pragmatic attitude towards Mexico's problems, and this meant abandoning the radical ideas of his predecessor.

Porfírio Díaz (1876-1910)

Díaz wanted to develop Mexico's economy, and he invited foreign investors to carry out the task. He was following the lead which Brazil, Chile and Argentina had given in changing their economies.

In 1870 Mexico's foreign trade was less than that of Peru; by 1910 it had increased by 100%, approaching £25 million a year. Díaz found one railway, from Mexico to Vera Cruz, in operation; by 1910 24,000 kilometres of track had been built. The mining of silver was revived in the 1880s and copper mining started in 1890. In the same year United States interests built up the Mexican Petroleum Company and began drilling for oil.

Díaz achieved material progress but he forgot the welfare of the mass of Mexicans, for the population rose from 9 million in 1870 to 13·5 million in 1900, implying the need for a vast programme of social reform, and this was neglected. An élite of intellectuals and businessmen called 'cientificos' carried out the President's programme. They were supposed to lead the way towards greater democracy, but in thirty-four years there was no sign that Díaz was prepared to let this happen. Díaz was a benevolent despot. Critics called his rule 'Díazpotism', though there was little terror during it. He employed army officers in political and administrative posts where they could not interfere with his own plans for government, and were free to make their fortunes. The conservative landowners, who also stood in opposition to him, were allowed to buy up public lands cheaply and evict Indian peasants from their holdings. Eight million square kilometres, a third of Mexico, was taken over in this way. Even the Church recovered some of its former possessions, Díaz allowing many of the anti-clerical laws of his former leader, Juárez, to lapse.

Mexico's government was changed by 'Porfirianismo', as the President's rule was called. Banditry was suppressed, budgets were balanced, investments soared, and Mexico was modernised. The majority of Mexicans were unaffected: only 5% gained any material benefits from Porfirianismo. The radicals could not hope to influence events by gaining power, as became more and more likely in Argentina, because there were not even the beginnings of a democratic system. Consequently Díaz's dictatorship was to end in revolution—the most important single revolution in modern Latin American history.

Uruguay (1829–1903)

Uruguay lacked political stability in the nineteenth century, but she can be associated in this chapter with the ABC states and Mexico, because her economic transformation matched theirs.

The smallest of the South American states owed its existence to the fact that both Argentina and Brazil wanted control of the Banda Oriental. In 1829, after years of Portuguese and Brazilian occupation, an independent state was established through British mediation. It was named the Oriental Republic of Uruguay. Both Argentina and Brazil continued to influence the internal politics of the young state where civil wars between rival factions were endemic. Indeed the two main factions 'Colorados', or Reds, and 'Blancos', or Whites, appealed for foreign help. After 1829 Rosas supported the Blancos, while Brazilians backed the Colorados. Uruguay found herself involved in the wider dispute between the Argentine dictator and the Anglo-French forces who blockaded the Río de la Plata. Montevideo, occupied by the Colorados and their allies, was besieged from 1843 until 1851 and became known as 'the new Troy'.

The fall of Rosas in 1852 did not free Uruguay from foreign entanglements because in the 1860s the issue of her independence became a cause of the war of the Triple Alliance. The Blanco government of Anatasio Aguirre was threatened by Colorado forces led by Venancio Flores. The Brazilians were prepared to make Flores President of Uruguay in return for a promise of support against Paraguay. Aguirre looked to the dictator of Paraguay, Francisco López, to prevent being overthrown. In August 1864, a Uruguayan gunboat was attacked by the Brazilians, and Uruguay subsequently invaded Brazil. In November 1864, Paraguay attacked Brazil, but was unable to prevent Flores being put into power in February 1865. Uruguay thereupon joined forces with Brazil, and Argentina completed the Triple Alliance against Paraguay in May 1865. Paraguay never attempted to interfere in Uruguayan politics again, but Brazil and Argentina exercised great influence on Uruguay, though her independent status was never threatened by them after this incident.

Economic changes (1870–1903)

Economic progress was difficult as long as Uruguay could not achieve internal stability. This came about through the determination of General Latorre to curb the local caudillos. He himself could still remark in 1880 that Uruguay was 'ungovernable', but in fact the interior provinces did begin to accept the rule of central government from Montevideo. Real stability was only achieved in this century.

Some degree of material progress had also taken place during the nineteenth century. As in Argentina conditions were very favourable and the three transforming agencies, immigration, foreign capital, and technological expertise, changed the land. The population rose from 30,000 in 1830 to 600,000 in 1870, to 950,000 in 1900, 150,000 of whom were European born. This scale of immigration was small in comparison to that in Brazil and Argentina, but larger than that of Chile, and it was relatively speaking just as significant. Foreign capital increased considerably in the 1880s and by 1902 almost £15 million were invested in railways, public utilities, and frigoríficos. Industrial technology also played its part. Montevideo was modernised, and public services were provided by British owned companies. It began to exercise great influence on the interior provinces where the small country towns were insignificant to comparison. Railway mileage increased from 309 kilometres in 1875 to 2,816 kilometres in 1895. When José Batlle y

Ordoñez, the creator of modern Uruguay, first became President in 1903 he noticed the significant changes since 1870. Uruguay was still a poor relation of Argentina and Brazil in economic terms, and she still had the largest public debt in South America, but foreign trade had doubled between 1870 and 1900, and her prosperity was as secure in the next fifty years as that of her neighbours.

Development in other states

A gap existed between the ABC states, Mexico and Uruguay and the other thirteen independent republics. These five states were the most developed. The other states had neither gained political stability nor enjoyed a continuous period of economic growth. The gap between the two groups of states can be shown by the fact that the combined foreign trade of Colombia and Venezuela in 1900 was less than that of Uruguay.

Paraguay

The third state occupying the Basin of the Río de la Plata, with Argentina and Uruguay, was Paraguay. In the years following independence it avoided the same type of civil disorder as Argentina and Uruguay had experienced by isolating itself from neighbours and adopting strong government.

For the first thirty years of independence José Francia ruled as an omnipotent President. He forbade foreign trade, imprisoned foreign travellers, and made Paraguay self sufficient. He was succeeded on his death in 1841 by Carlos López, who ruled until 1862. The new dictator reversed Francia's policy of isolation and encouraged foreigners to develop Paraguay. His son, Francisco López, who had little formal education, was made a Brigadier general at the age of eighteen, and at twenty-three boasted that he was a complete master of military tactics. In 1853, at the age of twenty-seven, he was sent to Europe to make Paraguay's existence known. While in Paris he acquired an Irish mistress, Eliza Lynch, who encouraged him to make his voice heard in the affairs of the Río de la Plata. The last words of Carlos López to his son were:

> There are many pending questions to ventilate; but do not try to solve them by the sword but by the pen, chiefly with Brazil.

Francisco López succeeded his father in 1862, and proceeded to ignore his advice. He could raise an army in excess of 100,000 by conscripting old men and boys, and this, together with the strong fortifications on the River Paraguay below Asuncíon, the capital, made him optimistic about the outcome of a war with Brazil and Argentina. When Brazil invaded Uruguay in support of the Colorado leader, Flores, López marched to attack Brazil in November 1864. He then demanded permission to pass through Argentine territory, and when refused he unwisely declared war against Argentina (March 1865). Uruguay had already joined Brazil, and in May 1865 they formed the Triple Alliance to fight Paraguay. The war lasted five years, ending only with the hunting down and death of López on March 1st, 1870.

Paraguayans have always regarded the dictator who led them into the war, and kept at bay the combined forces of three states for five years, as a hero. One writer, Juan O'Leary, whose relatives were tortured by López, wrote:

> His cyclopean figure has remained alone but firmly set on its high pedestal, defying the hurricane of passion and the destructive action of time.

Other writers have come nearer the truth when they speak of the dictator's cruelty and megalomania:

> Among the tyrant's victims, one counts hundreds of distinguished women and young ladies, whose only crime was in being mothers, wives, daughters or sisters of supposed conspirators.

These are the words of a Paraguayan historian, Cecilio Báez, describing López's furious reaction to defeat. The price of one man's ambition was disastrous for Paraguay.

The war ruined Paraguay—she lost 143,000 square kilometres of territory to Argentina and Brazil, half her population of five hundred thousand were killed, and only twenty-eight thousand men remained alive in 1871. López was supposed to have said just before his death: 'Muero con mi patria'—'I die with my country' —and its devastation was so complete that this is scarcely an exaggeration. By 1900 Paraguay had barely started to recover from

Part of a monument at Mendoza, Argentina, showing
San Martín setting out to cross the Andes

the war, and it was not until 1932 that the population losses had been made good.

Bolivia

Paraguay suffered tragically from a war of her own making, but Bolivia was more unfortunate. The War of the Pacific (1879-1883), described on page 80, cost Bolivia her only coast line, and undermined national morale. Bolivia's dictators were perhaps not as fanatical as López, but were certainly as corrupt. Only President Santa Cruz (1828-1838), who briefly united Peru and Bolivia together, was capable of ruling the new land effectively. A succession of rulers followed him, culminating in the cruel and violent presidency of Mariano Melgarejo (1864-1871). Elections were rigged, army officers manoeuvred for power, and the treasury was periodically ransacked. The War of the Pacific meant the loss of nitrate deposits, and one positive result was that the Bolivians were awakened to the need to develop other sources of wealth. In the 1880s the production of tin began on a large scale, rising from 1,000 tons a year to 15,000 tons a year in 1905. There was also a short lived rubber 'boom' in the forest areas to the north. But these signs of economic progress and development were not longstanding. In 1903 part of the area of rubber production, Acre, was lost to Brazil. The army continued to be the arbiter of politics, and in 1900 Bolivia was very backward, underpopulated, and seriously divided. Probably no more than one-tenth of the estimated population of 1,700,000 were involved in the nation's political affairs.

Peru

Peru's experience was different from that of Bolivia. She enjoyed a period of prosperity during the rule of Ramón Castilla (1845-1862), when the export of guano, which lay thickly on the offshore islands, found a ready market in Europe and brought handsome profits. But reckless expenditure on railway construction in the Andes led to bankruptcy. The War of the Pacific (1879-1883) revealed the weaknesses of Peru—Lima was occupied for a number of years by Chilean forces, and it took many years for the country to recover.

A monument in Montevideo to the opening up of the Pampa

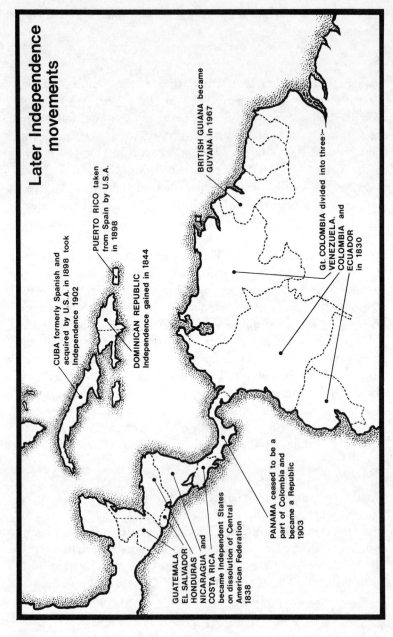

Later Independence movements

CUBA formerly Spanish and acquired by U.S.A. in 1898 took Independence 1902

PUERTO RICO taken from Spain by U.S.A. in 1898

DOMINICAN REPUBLIC Independence gained in 1844

BRITISH GUIANA became GUYANA in 1967

Gt. COLOMBIA divided into three:— VENEZUELA, COLOMBIA and ECUADOR in 1830

GUATEMALA EL SALVADOR HONDURAS NICARAGUA and COSTA RICA became Independent States on dissolution of Central American Federation 1838

PANAMA ceased to be a part of Colombia and became a Republic 1903

Only in the 1890s did the mines begin to make profits again, when revenue was wisely invested in education and agriculture. Peru, which had been richer than Mexico in 1870, was thirty years later an undeveloped, underpopulated state in which the Indian majority was excluded from public life.

Ecuador

Further north the three states which had comprised Bolívar's Gran Colombia (1822-1830) all experienced brief periods of stability which did not lead to any long lived economic expansion. Ecuador suffered from the constant rivalry between the Pacific port of Guayaquil and the Andean capital of Quito. The one notable ruler was García Moreno (1860-1875), who established a theocratic state. He also built roads and schools, and commenced the construction of the railway between Quito and Guayaquil. At the end of the century cacao was the one product which Ecuador could export. Her political system seemed to be as backward as that of her Andean neighbours to the south: a small creole élite ruled the mass of Indians and mestizos.

Colombia

Colombia and Venezuela both suffered from military rule for long periods but otherwise their experiences were very different. García Calderón wrote that 'In Colombia men have fought for ideas' and pointed to two main areas of dispute: centralism versus federalism, the rivalry between Bogotá and the other departments; and Church versus state, the rivalry between anti-clerical liberals and conservative traditionalists.

Francisco Santander, Bolívar's able vice-President, became the first President of Colombia, or New Granada as it was first known, in 1832. He tried to conciliate liberals and conservatives, and for five years succeeded. His followers continued the process with less success, until in 1848 civil war broke out. It continued intermittently for thirty years until the emergence of Rafael Nuñez, known as the 'Regenerator' by conservatives, and a dictator by liberals. Between 1874 and 1894 he provided order and stability, during which time economic advance might have taken place. In the years immediately after independence Colombia had seemed one of the most stable republics. There seemed to be no apparent reason why the country could not have been developed economically, but such a possibility had vanished in the disorders after 1848. Forty years later Nuñez was more interested in restoring clerical privileges and centralising the government than in material progress. On his death in 1894 political instability returned, and the bloody civil war (1899-1902) cost one hundred thousand lives. It was followed by the loss of Panama in 1903.

Venezuela

Colombia's instability was no greater than that of Venezuela, the birthplace of the Liberator Simón Bolívar, which was ruled at the turn of the century by the illiterate and corrupt President Cipriano Castro. He followed a long line of caudillos of whom the most notable had been Bolívar's old lieutenant, José Páez (1830-1846). Páez had tried to restore the devastation left by the Wars of Emancipation, and encourage agriculture and immigration, but in 1850 Venezuela's population was still the same as it had been forty years earlier—which was 800,000.

One other dictator, Guzmán Blanco (1870-1888), stands out as a ruler efficient and strong enough to lay the foundations for material progress. He built railways and roads, expanded coffee production and increased foreign investment. Blanco, however, built up a personal fortune to support himself should events force him out of power, periodically plundering the national exchequer in order to do so. Once ousted from power by a revolution during his absence in Europe, he made no attempt to risk his life by returning to Venezuela. Blanco has been compared to Díaz in Mexico. Both were pragmatic rulers and both tried to preserve a façade of liberalism for their dictatorships. But whereas Díazpotism did transform and modernise Mexico's economy, the result of Blanco's rule was negative. He merely set an example of corruption which others, for example Cipriano Castro, who were less able than himself, followed.

Central America

The political history of the Central American Republics in the nineteenth century is the story of attempts to re-establish federal government, which had collapsed in 1838. The region was a politically unstable one, in which the small states quarrelled with one another, and were beset by threats of interference and fears of conquests.

Guatemala enjoyed a certain predominance, and exercised influence over the governments of her two neighbours, Honduras and El Salvador. Nicaragua was ruled by the North American filibuster, William Walker, for a brief period (1855–1857), and had to recognise a British protectorate over the Mosquito Coast until 1860. Costa Rica, the fifth state of the original Federation, avoided the worst excesses of its northern neighbours and advanced towards a democratic system. It held the first free elections in the area in 1889, long before many South American states did.

Economically the five republics made little progress. The first company to invest on a large scale in Central America, the North American United Fruit Company, only began to do so in Costa Rica in 1899, and thus in the nineteenth century there was little commercial exploitation of the foodstuffs grown in the area. In 1900 coffee and bananas headed the list of exports in all the five states, but Uruguay's wealth exceeded that of the whole region.

Hispaniola

Two other independent republics existed in Latin America, both occupying one island. Haiti, the former French negro colony, occupied the western third of the island of Hispaniola, and the Dominican Republic the other part. The Haitians had become independent in 1803, leading the way for the rest of Latin America, but their progress since has been marked by disorder and violence. Between 1843 and 1915 Haiti had twenty-two dictators.

The Dominicans were controlled by Haiti for twenty-two years, until in 1844 they set up their own creole republic. But they showed little inclination to keep their new independence. Between 1861 and 1865 Spain renewed her control of the Dominicans by their

CHAPTER SIX

Trade Table: 1900
VALUES IN MILLIONS OF U.S. DOLLARS

	IMPORTS	EXPORTS	TOTAL TRADE
BRAZIL (1901)	22.5	43.0	65.5
ARGENTINA	22.7	30.9	53.6
CUBA (1901)	13.3	12.1	25.4
CHILE	9.6	12.5	22.1
MEXICO	6.1	15.8	21.9
URUGUAY	5.1	6.3	11.4
PERU (1902)	3.4	3.7	7.1
COLOMBIA (1898)	2.2	3.8	6.0
VENEZUELA	1.9	3.2	5.1
BOLIVIA (1901)	1.4	3.1	4.5
ECUADOR (1901)	1.5	1.7	3.2
GUATEMALA (1902)	0.8	1.8	2.6
DOMINICAN R.	0.7	1.2	1.9
COSTA RICA	0.8	0.8	1.6
EL SALVADOR	0.5	0.8	1.3
PARAGUAY	0.4	0.4	0.8
NICARAGUA (1902)	0.5	0.3	0.8
HONDURAS	0.4	0.4	0.8
PANAMA (1903)	0.5	0.2	0.7

No figures obtainable for HAITI

own invitation, and thereafter, on a number of occasions, Dominicans offered to sell part or all of their island to the United States. Dictators ruled as tyrants until the United States intervened in 1915 in Haiti, and 1916 in the Dominican Republic, to provide political and economic stability there.

Cuba

Cuba remained a Spanish colony for the whole of the nineteenth century, but to Spain it proved to be only a drain into which money and men were poured to fight never-ending guerilla wars. Twice Cuba fought unsuccessfully for independence, in the Ten Years War (1868–1878), and in the unsuccessful revolt of 1895–1896. In 1898 the United States intervened to assist Cuba in her fight for independence. The Spanish authorities were blamed for the sinking of a United States warship, *S. S. Maine*. A war between the United States and Spain followed, which resulted in the independence of Cuba and Puerto Rica. A new era began in the Caribbean in which the United States appeared as both the chief benefactor and the chief aggressor.

Cuba had prospered until 1895. Foreign trade totalled £30 million, and it was the destruction of her sugar estates during the war of independence which halted her economic progress thereafter. But for this, Cuba could have been added to the five other Latin American states mentioned which had made real economic progress by the end of the nineteenth century.

Conclusion

The political and economic conditions in most states seemed depressingly similar, after almost a century of independence, to the years immediately after the wars of independence: caudillos still ruled, civil wars still raged, liberals still quarrelled with conservatives, and federalists with centralists. But to the outside observer the picture was not quite so gloomy everywhere. One can recall the optimism of as acute an observer as the British statesman James Bryce who, writing in 1912 of Argentina, said:

> Though no doubt there is an ostentatious display of wealth, work is more abundant, wages are higher than in any part of the world.

The twentieth century: the challenge to the old order

The struggle to break the power of the caudillos and establish a stable government which would provide the right conditions for economic expansion dominated the history of the nineteenth century in Latin America.

The majority of countries were not democracies in 1900; a few were constitutional republics, most were dictatorships, but all were controlled by small groups of landowners and businessmen. These oligarchies ruled with the aid of foreign investors, and achieved their position through show of force rather than by election. The Latin American states each produced one or two mineral and agricultural commodities, which they sold at prices determined by a fluctuating world demand. In return they bought manufactured goods from western Europe and the United States: they were dependent on the outside world, both politically and economically.

In this century the power of the established oligarchies has been threatened. Few states have escaped revolutionary developments, which have either overthrown the existing order or forced fundamental reform on the Latin American governments. The two most extreme forms of rebellion were the Mexican Revolution of 1910 and the Cuban Revolution which began in 1959. These events in Latin America will be more easily understood if they are placed in the context of world history in the twentieth century. Four events have dominated world affairs in this century: World War I, the Depression, World War II, and the ideological conflict between communism and the West. World War I (1914-1918) marked the highpoint of the alliance between the ruling classes and foreign business interests, which had brought about the economic transformation of parts of Latin America during the nineteenth century.

After World War I, the 'golden' era of prosperity in Argentina, Chile, and Brazil never returned.

The 1920s were years of great difficulty for all Latin America. Foreign investments declined, European markets shrank, and the prices of the mineral and agricultural commodities which the continent could supply to the rest of the world fell catastrophically. The Depression of 1929 merely underlined these alarming facts. Reactions were twofold. On the political front the old caudillos returned to power in alliance with the conservatives. Only Costa Rica and Colombia avoided dictatorships during the Depression years; elsewhere democracy was temporarily defeated and radical parties which had gained power in the 1920s lost it for as long as a quarter of a century.

Criticism arising from a certain resentment of foreign capitalism was stimulated by the years of the Depression. As a result, demands for self sufficiency and tariff protection increased and continued during the years of World War II (1939-1945). Admiration for German and Italian militarism led to the growth of authoritarian governments in the 1930s, which continued in power in most states until the 1950s, and under them economic nationalism took on a new emphasis as major foreign interests, like the oil fields in Mexico and railways in Argentina, were taken over by governments.

The ideological dispute between communism and the West which has dominated world affairs since 1945 first appeared to enter the Latin American sphere of politics in 1962, when the 'Missile Crisis' brought world attention to Cuba. It had, however, affected the continent much earlier. The action of the United States in intervening in Guatemala in 1954, to prevent a left-wing government continuing in power, is one example. The view of the United States taken by Latin Americans, as either the fairy godmother supplying large amounts of capital, or the wicked stepmother with her imperialist designs, results from both her attitude towards communism and the ambivalence of Latin Americans towards their powerful northern neighbour.

The demand for change has accelerated in Latin America particularly since World War II, and the necessity for it is plain for all to see. The challenge to the old order began this century in 1903 when Batlle first became President of Uruguay, though attempts had been made before this event to bring about radical reforms, without success. The movement of La Reforma, led by Juárez, in Mexico promised a social revolution, as we have seen, but Díaz failed to complete the process, and the authority of the oligarchy remained untouched. Radicalism was a growing force in Chilean and Argentinian politics in the 1890s, but at that time it had no effect on their respective governments' policies.

In the last seventy years almost every state has been affected by pressure for greater democracy and the wider distribution of the national wealth. In some countries radical change was achieved without violence, notably in the ABC states and Uruguay. In others a civil war was necessary, the Mexican Revolution being the most famous among them. Some attempts at revolution have failed, like those in Guatemala and Bolivia, and the revolution in Cuba is continuing.

This chapter sets out to examine the main changes that have taken place in Latin America in this century in three ways. First it outlines the developments in the six countries, Argentina, Brazil, Mexico, Chile, Uruguay, and Cuba, which were the most prosperous in 1900. Secondly, an attempt is made to trace the causes and consequences of revolutions in two of the most backward countries, Bolivia and Guatemala. Finally, a summary is made of the histories of the other twelve republics, placing an emphasis on their present economic and political situation.

Argentina (1916–1971)

In 1914 Argentina, the most powerful independent state of Latin America, was spoken of in the same breath as the United States. She seemed poised on the threshold of even greater productivity and prosperity than that which she had achieved during the nineteenth century, the main obstacle being the need to accept the immigrants as first class Argentinians.

In 1912 President Saenz Peña had introduced the Reform Bill which bears his name. It allowed all males over the age of eighteen to have 'a free secret and obligatory' vote, and led directly to the radical party winning the 1916 election.

Hipólito Irigoyen and the Radicals (1916-1930)

The first Radical President, Hipólito Irigoyen (1916–1922), dominated the next fourteen years of Argentine politics. He was already sixty-four years old when he was elected. Neither an estanciero nor an army officer, Irigoyen had been a harsh critic of the conservative oligarchy, and its failure to carry out reforms. He proceeded to adopt more radical policies. He set up a national organisation to develop the oil deposits found in Patagonia, rather than allow foreign companies to exploit such resources. He also passed social reforms, designed to reduce hours of labour, and distribute land more evenly. But these policies fell short of a fundamental change in the economic and social structure of Argentina. Though the middle classes increased their power, the landowning oligarchy remained the masters.

Irigoyen established Radical control of national and provincial politics, but split his own party in the process in 1922, an action which was to have important repercussions in the next forty years. In the 1928 election he was triumphantly returned for a second term as President, but this proved disastrous for him. Irigoyen was incapable of dealing with the growing effects of the world Depression. He clung jealously to power and was finally ousted from office by a military coup d'état on September 6th, 1930.

The military-conservative rule (1930-1943)

For the first time since the era of Rosas the armed forces controlled Argentina. They continued to do so until one of their number, Colonel Perón, who had been present at the military coup in 1930, organised a popular movement to win power. The 1930s witnessed a return to the conservative rule of landowners supported by the military. The main opposition party, the Radicals, were split, and supporters of Irigoyen were prevented from standing for public office. At first the 1853 constitution was respected and elections took place. A coalition, formed in 1931, dominated by conservatives, proceeded to elect an army officer, Agustín Justo, President (1931-1937). He gradually eroded the democratic framework of society: fraud and intimidation dominated elections, and though Irigoyen's record in this respect had been worse, privacy and freedom completely disappeared under Justo.

Justo also restored Argentina to her traditional dependence on Britain. The Roca-Runciman Treaty of 1933 safeguarded the British market for Argentine beef, and in return Britain was able to control 85% of all the frigoríficos in the Republic, and gain preferential terms for industrial exports. It is difficult to see what alternative Justo had, when the economy of Argentina was in a weakened position, but the treaty was highly unpopular among the more radical Argentines. At a time when democratic forces were being penalised and divided, and when Europe was turning towards totalitarian governments, the Roca-Runciman Treaty encouraged the growth of a nationalist movement which demanded strong authoritarian leadership.

Roberto Ortiz succeeded Justo as President, but ill-health forced him to effectively retire in 1940, and with him the last hope for a restoration of constitutional rule ended.

His vice President, Ramón Castillo, was sympathetic to the Axis powers in World War II, and Argentina adopted first a neutralist position, and then an openly pro-Hitler position. This proved to be an error of political judgement. While Argentina remained hostile to the United States and Britain, Brazil received 'lend lease' aid for her support of the Allies. All other Latin American states pressed for the breaking off of relations with the Axis powers, and Argentina was isolated. Castillo himself was surrounded by plotters. On June 4th, 1943, a group of army generals and colonels, including Castillo's war minister Pedro Ramírez, and Colonel Perón, seized power. The officer clique called itself the Group of United Officers, and the coup seemed merely a repetition of General Uriburu's seizure of power in 1930.

In 1943 Argentina bore scant resemblance to the country in 1914. Industrialisation had taken place to the extent that manufactures exceeded agricultural products in value, and the urban population outnumbered the rural population by three to one. Buenos Aires was, next to New York, the greatest urban concentration in the Americas. The Depression of 1929 had two important effects on the population: it led to rural unemployment, which encouraged migration to the towns, and it ended foreign immigration. In 1914 greater Buenos Aires had a population of 2 million, in 1937 3·5 million, and in 1947 4·75 million. Immigrants, who had composed 1 million in 1914, only numbered 1·25 million in 1947, whereas internal migrants increased from 200 thousand to 1·5 million during the same period. The migrants were a discontented group. They became known as the 'Descamisados', which means shirtless ones; and Colonel Perón saw their value as a popular support in his rise to power.

In 1943 all the officers who had taken part in the coup were agreed on the need for military control of the government, but there was a disagreement over how to ensure this control. Ramírez and the traditional officers favoured a right wing alliance with the Catholic Church and the landowners, which would have preserved the century-old traditional bases of Argentine society. Perón saw that this proposal was unrealistic. He argued that Uriburu and the army officers had failed to preserve power after the 1930 revolution precisely because he failed to gain popular support. Perón began to organise the Descamisados into a para-military trade union, the Confederación General de Trabajadores (CTG).

Perón's rise to power (1943-1946)

Juan Domingo Perón was born in 1895 in the province of Buenos Aires. In 1911 he entered military school to train as an officer, and at the time of the 1930 coup he had reached the position of major. He showed tremendous interest in social studies and history, writing books and articles on the subjects. In 1938 he visited Europe as a military observer with the Italian army, and was deeply impressed by Mussolini's Fascist state.

These impressions strengthened his conviction that there must be an alliance between the military and organised labour if real change were to be brought about in Argentina. After the coup in

Perón with his wife, Eva Duarte in 1952

Getuliò Vargas, 1883–1954, President of Brazil

June 1943, Perón was appointed to the Ministry of War, and in October 1943 to the headship of the Ministry of Labour and Social Security. He worked assiduously. He built up support within the armed services, and he promised the workers higher wages if they would join the CGT. In December 1943 he made the annual payment of one month's salary, as a Christmas bonus, compulsory, thus gaining popularity in the working classes. When war ended in Europe in May 1945, Perón's position was strong but by no means secure. Democratic forces had triumphed over fascism and nazism, and the clamour for a return to constitutional government in Argentina grew.

Perón, with his fascist sympathies, was an obvious target for an attack by the liberal opposition. On October 9th, 1945, he was arrested and imprisoned on an island in the Plate estuary. Perón's supporters proposed a demonstration in protest, and led by a woman, Eva Duarte, they threatened to riot unless he was released. General Farrell's military government bowed before this threat of civil disorder and Perón was released on October 17th, 1945. Perón resigned his government offices and his colonel's commission, and declared his intention to stand for the presidency.

I have resigned from the army in order to help revive the almost forgotten civilian traditions of Argentina, and join with the sweating, suffering mass of labourers who are building the greatness of this nation.

He married Eva Duarte, who became popularly known as Evita, and the scene was set for his bid for power.

He offered a clear programme of sweeping social reforms, while the opposition forces bickered and argued. At the same time the United States' State Department published a Blue Book which cited the collaboration of leading Argentines with the Axis powers. This move was particularly ill-timed. Perón complained of 'Yanqui' interference in Argentine elections, and won a clear majority over his rival, José Tamborini. The election was by all accounts relatively free and honest, and Perón won because of the solid support he received from the Descamisados, many of whom were voting for the first time.

Perón in power (1946-1955)

Perón rapidly established an authoritarian regime. With the opposition parties silenced, the universities muzzled, and a revised constitution in 1948, which gave him increased executive powers, Perón could be expected to be re-elected. Criticism of government officials became a criminal offence and Perón's doctrine of 'Justicialismo' became official. Justicialismo was an attempt to give coherence to three ideas of Perón: nationalism, social justice and economic independence. It suggested that Perón had found a third course between capitalism and communism.

Perón proceeded to carry out social reform. He relied strongly on his wife Evita's support, and his demise was rapid after her death in 1952. The year 1949 probably marked the high point of his nine years in power, and in the first three years of his presidency he seemed to be achieving his declared aims. First, he set out to nationalise foreign owned businesses and make Argentina economically independent. He bought foreign owned railways, steamship lines and public utilities, paying generous compensation—£120 million to Britain alone.

Secondly, he was determined to increase industrialisation. Between 1946 and 1949 manufactures increased by 31% and the Gross National Product of all goods and services reached a total of 62·3 billion pesos in 1948, compared with 47·6 billion in 1945.

Thirdly, Perón was determined to restore Argentina's international prestige, which was badly tarnished by her policies during World War II. He made Argentina the champion of Latin America against foreign interference, adopting the now familiar neutralist third position between the Soviet Union and the United States. In 1948 Perón offered financial aid to the rest of Latin America, which the United States, preoccupied with her Marshall Aid Programme in Europe, appeared to be ignoring.

Perón's policies were helped by Argentina's favourable balance of trade. During World War II there had been a ready market for her foodstuffs in Europe, where demand always outstripped supply, and Argentina accumulated large reserves of currency which she could now spend. Some of the surplus was spent buying foreign interests (about £200 million worth), but most of it was used to satisfy wage demands. The Descamisados received regular wage increases, their real wages rising by 34% between 1946 and 1949. Perón gained supporters who have never forgotten those years of plenty, but the long term effect of this inflationary policy was disastrous. Agriculture was neglected, the government paid low prices for meat and wheat, but sold these products abroad at higher prices, taking the profits for itself. State control of railways and other public services did not increase efficiency, but only the labour force. Perón's promised steel plant, to rival that of Brazil, never materialised, while factories flooded the market with inferior consumer goods which might well have been imported. Inflation became rampant, and the foreign currency reserves dwindled.

In 1950 an economic depression began. Within two years the Gross National Product had fallen to 49·3 billion pesos, meat was rationed, and wheat was being imported; industry lacked power, raw materials and spare parts for machinery; communications were completely inadequate. Perón had either to adopt more realistic policies or face economic disaster. He reversed his economic policy; workers' wage demands were refused; and a United States company was granted oil drilling concessions. He dealt with unrest by firmly taking command of the armed services.

As the country faced austerity, Perón was determined to hang on to power at all costs. His personal authority was increased in 1952 when he was re-elected as President, supported by a suppliant congress, which bestowed on him the title of 'Liberator of the Republic'. In the following year Perón began to appoint all university rectors, thus ending the little freedom they had enjoyed since 1948. But the event which finally undermined the dictator's popular support took place in 1954. He had tried to get the Roman Catholic Church to canonise Eva Perón for her social work, without success, and so he began a systematic persecution of the Church. Crucifixes and images were replaced by busts of Eva Perón, and religious teaching in schools was suspended. Justicialismo was made a compulsory part of the school curriculum. In 1955 Perón attempted to extend the teaching of this doctrine to the armed services. When an abortive military revolt took place in June 1955, the President reacted by threatening violence. On August 31st he addressed a mass rally:

> He who in any place tries to disturb ˙order in opposition to the constituted authorities or contrary to the law or the constitution, may be slain by any Argentine.

On September 7th his massive CGT union called for arms to form a 6 million strong para-military force in defence of Perón. The military waited no more. An army revolt started in Cordoba on September 16th, and the navy threatened to bombard Buenos Aires unless Perón surrendered within three days. The President fled to the safety of Paraguay.

The legacy of Perón (1955–1971)

Sixteen years after Perón's fall Argentina is still under his spell. His one notable achievement was to bring about a social and economic revolution which benefited the urban working classes. The traditional power of the estanciero oligarchy was broken, and the unfulfilled revolution of Irigoyen was completed. Perón's title 'Liberator of the Republic' was an echo of one of his heroes, Rosas. His popular nationalism was reminiscent of that of the nineteenth century caudillo.

During the last sixteen years two rival groups have really commanded the political stage. On the one side the 'Peronistas', entrenched in the trade unions, have condemned all that has happened since as a betrayal of Perón's revolution. On the other hand, the anti-Peronista officers have remained as determined as ever in their opposition to any return either of the ageing dictator or his policies. The result has been an unsettled period for Argentina.

Until May 1958 a military junta ruled. It declared the 'Peronista' party illegal and the CGT was purged of members. In 1958 civilian rule was restored, the Radical Arturo Frondizi being elected president, but only because he was supported by Peronistas who could not themselves put forward a candidate. Frondizi's position was therefore delicate, and his attempt to keep on good terms with both Peronistas and the anti-Peronista officers failed. In 1962

Frondizi, prompted by the army, intervened to cancel a victory the Peronistas had won in the congressional elections. This was the first occasion the Peronistas had had of putting forward their candidate, and it merely demonstrated the support which the ex-President and his policies still commanded. Frondizi did not survive long. In March 1962 he was overthrown and replaced by a new military junta. New elections in July 1963 led to the appointment of Arturo Illia, a leader of the main Radical group, as president. The Peronistas were not allowed to contest the election. Dr Illia failed to 'heal the nation's wounds', to use his own words, and in the Congressional elections of 1965 the Peronistas were again allowed to stand, and won 31% of the votes. They were still outnumbered in Congress by Illia's Radicals, but the military were not prepared to stand aside any longer.

In June 1966 the armed forces, led by General Juan Onganía, seized power, and on June 8th 1970 he was overthrown by other officers in a bloodless coup d'état. The military regimes have been trying to find grass roots of Argentina's problems. Far-reaching reforms have been introduced including a much needed reduction of government employees. The peso was devalued by 40% in 1967 to make Argentina more competitive, and agriculture has been reinvigorated by investment. But inflation continues at the rate of 30% a year and this could undermine these realistic policies. The shadow of Perón, now exiled in Spain, still haunts Argentina.

Brazil (1889-1971)

Brazil's established tradition of stable government and economic prosperity continued under the Republic which was set up after the deposition of Pedro II. Brazil's history this century closely parallels that of Argentina. Both rapidly expanded until World War I, and then were hard hit by the effects of the Depression. The military have since dominated the two states, both Perón and the resilient President Vargas depending on their backing; and in the last fifteen years chronic inflation has hit both states very severely. But whereas Argentina has made little overall progress since the Depression, Brazil's achievements have been considerable.

For twenty-five years after 1889 the coffee 'barons' dominated political and economic life. The abolition of slavery was more than offset by the influx of immigrants—there were about 3 million during these years, most settling in the states of São Paulo and Minas Gerais. The production of coffee expanded until Brazil provided three-quarters of the world's output in 1914. The market was flooded, and steps were taken to withhold supplies until the world market improved. There was also a short lived rubber boom. In 1910 Brazil dominated the world rubber market, and the port of Manaos, 1,600 kilometres up the Amazon river, had become as a result a great city with an internationally famous opera house. The dreams of an equatorial paradise for fortune hunters seemed near realisation. But within twenty years the boom was ended, and the plantations in Malaya, built up from seeds smuggled out of Brazil by the Englishman, Henry Wickam, captured the world market in rubber.

Foreign immigration and investment continued unabated during the period. One area which benefited particularly was the State of São Paulo. The city of São Paulo grew from a population of 35,000 in 1883 to 500,000 in 1917, and to 1 million in 1930. The state produced two-thirds of the nation's coffee, had a rail network second only to Buenos Aires in intensity, and attracted most of Brazil's foreign investment. Professor Johnson has described the state as being like 'a locomotive pulling twenty empty box cars'— the other states. The neighbouring state of Minas Gerais also benefited from the boom, and the two states shared power. They produced the Presidents alternatively—one year a Paulista, the next a Miniero.

The first sign of impending crisis came when the government resorted in 1922 to limiting the export of coffee until the world market improved. But production of coffee continued at a high level, and when in October 1929 the world price of coffee collapsed, producers and merchants were ruined. Wider repercussions followed in 1930. Exports fell by one-third, foreign credits dried up, and millions of tons of coffee were burnt or thrown into the sea. Popular frustration turned on the government which had failed to reduce coffee production and diversify the economy. The ruling President, Washington Luis, was a Paulista who had broken precedent by supporting a fellow Paulista, Carlos Prestes, to succeed him. Prestes won the election of 1930, but was accused of dishonesty. The army seized power and the rival candidate, Getúlio Vargas, was made President in November, 1930.

Vargas and the Estado Novo (1930-1945)

Getúlio Vargas represented the southern state of Rio Grande do Sul, and as such challenged the traditional supremacy of Minas Gerais and São Paulo. The army officers who had supported him expected him to be a conservative who would continue to rule on behalf of the 'coffee orientated colonial economy'. Vargas was not prepared to be anybody's puppet. The military junta had made him provisional President and he promised elections for a Constituent Assembly. In November 1932 the Constituent Assembly met and elected Vargas president for four years, 1934-1938. It also agreed to a new constitution which increased restrictions on foreigners. As Vargas' term of office ended he announced another new constitution. This was to be put into effect when it had been approved by a national plebiscite, and in the interim period Vargas was empowered to rule by decree. This manoeuvre by Vargas was designed simply so that he could hold onto power, for the plebiscite was never held. In the next eight years Vargas ruled as dictator, supported by the approving nods of Hitler and Mussolini. But his government was not a prelude to European style totalitarian government. Vargas called his dictatorship the 'Estado Novo', the New State, and promised to introduce reform. Foreigners were penalised and more severely restricted. A mixed economy evolved, but with the state providing more and more of the capital for new enterprises. Trade unions were legalised and social security introduced. The Estado Novo adopted European ideas of the corporate state.

Unlike the Argentines, however, Vargas did not criticise the United States on entering World War II. He supported the North Americans, and shrewdly offered them the use of Brazil's airfields.

In 1942 Brazil herself entered the war, and began to benefit from the Lend Lease aid which the United States was prepared to give any allied country, and this caused much annoyance to Argentina. Vargas began to diversify the economy, and develop industry. A steel plant—the first in Latin America—was built at Volta Redonda, a symbol of Brazilian nationalism and a necessary base for heavy industry. With the increasing political stability at the end of the war, there was no doubt that Brazil was the pre-eminent power in South America. Vargas seemed inclined to allow civilian rule to return to Brazil, and fixed elections for December 1945. The army thought that Vargas' actions were merely a prelude to a new manoeuvre to enable him to hold onto power, and forced him to resign in October 1945.

Post-War Brazil (1945-1971)

Vargas was returned to Congress as the Senator for the state of Río Grande do Sul and continued to exercise great political influence. The new President, General Dutra (1945-1950), a former Minister of War under Vargas, continued to carry out the same blend of nationalist politics. His rule proved to be merely a brief interlude before the return of the senator from the Río Grande do Sul to the presidency in 1950.

Vargas had tremendous popular support in 1950, and everyone looked to him for a repetition of the economic successes of the Estado Novo. There was no triumphal return. He allowed corruption and nepotism a free hand. He failed to check xenophobic nationalists, who frightened off foreign investors and consequently prevented the proper development of Brazil's oil reserves. He also lost control of demogogues within his own government, like the young Minister of Labour, João Goulart, while his electoral promise of free institutions proved mythical. In 1954 a shooting incident took place. The victim, Carlos Lacerda, was a newspaper editor and a fierce critic of the President, who had persisted in publishing attacks on the government while others remained silent. Vargas was implicated in the incident, and he was pressed to resign. A few days later on August 24th, Getúlio Vargas shot himself.

The President's policies had created a more balanced economy which had allowed a middle class to emerge to bridge the gap between the peasants and the coffee barons. This was achieved without the benefit of massive surpluses such as Perón had inherited in 1946. The two men were, however, strikingly similar. They both built up popular support in the previously forgotten working classes; they both changed the traditional structure of society; and they both created situations which their successors have never escaped from. Vargas' achievements seemed on balance to have been more worthwhile, but he left his follower, Juscelino Kubitschek, a devalued cruzeiro and inflation to deal with.

Kubitschek (1956–1960) embarked on an ambitious programme to bring Brazil 'fifty years progress in five'. He needed massive foreign investment, but as the political heir of Vargas he could not afford to be seen pandering to foreigners. He began an extravagant plan to move the capital from Río de Janeiro to the interior in an attempt to start a new era of development in Brazil. In 1956 the Brazilian Congress agreed to the building of Brasilia.

Brasilia is a monument to Brazil's belief in the future, and at the same time a reason for some of its economic troubles. Kubitschek's policy led to a spiralling cost of living and unchecked inflation. His answer was to print more money, but by 1959 he had to further devalue the cruzeiro. His successors, Jânio Quadros (1961–1962) and Goulart (1962–1964), failed to check the economic slide. Goulart in particular followed an unrealistic leftist policy which made little economic sense. Prices in the shops rose daily and foreigners were not allowed to take any profits out of the country.

The army, which had kept out of politics since 1945, feared that Goulart was on the point of establishing a Cuban style of dictatorship, and took control in 1964, sending Goulart into exile.

Brazil's military rulers have since brought more and more civilians into the government. They have restored overseas confidence in Brazil's credibility, but scarcely faced the problem of the poor areas of the country, and the growing demands for a return to constitutional rule. The parallel with Argentina is again apt. The legacy of Vargas continues to overshadow Brazilian politics.

Mexico (1910–1971)

Brazil's recent history, like Argentina's, has been confused by the actions of a popular dictator. It would have been difficult to forecast such events before the great Depression. In Mexico the picture is clearer because the first changes in government took place over fifty years ago, and a pattern of gradual evolution has since emerged.

In 1908 Porfirio Díaz unwittingly announced to a North American journalist, James Creelman, that he would not stand again for re-election, and a campaign was launched by two progressive landowners, Francisco and Gustavo Madero, to make sure that he kept his word. Díaz arrested Francisco, but confident of his position, soon released him. In 1910 Díaz was easily re-elected in a rigged election, and the Maderos called for a national revolution to begin on November 20th. The movement started in the north and a supporting revolt led by Emiliano Zapata also broke out in the south. Zapata advanced upon Mexico City whereupon Díaz panicked and fled.

The Revolution

The Maderos soon lost control of the forces that had brought them to power, and thereafter the Mexican Revolution proved to be a crucible for the conflicting ideas of revolutionary leaders competing for control. There were four outstanding leaders: Zapata, an Indian from Guerrero who campaigned under the slogan 'Land for the landless', a direct echo of Juárez; Venustiano Carranza, Governor of Coahuila; his ally Alvaro Obregón; and the most famous bandit of all time, 'Pancho' Villa.

Zapata would not accept the rule of the Maderos and continued his attacks on estates in the south. Civil war broke out all over the country. Victoriano Huerta, Francisco Madero's commander-in-chief, taking advantage of the confusion, seized power on February 18th, 1913. The Maderos were shot and Huerta proceeded to try to restore the tranquility and order of Porfirio Díaz's regime. He was supported by H. L. Wilson, the United States ambassador, who told the diplomatic corps in Mexico City: 'Mexico has been saved. From now on we shall have peace, progress and prosperity.'

Contemporary mural of Zapata by Diego Rivera

Carranza then demanded a restoration of the constitutional government, which the Maderos had attempted to introduce, and marched on Mexico City. Villa joined him, while Zapata moved in from the south. The new President of the United States, Woodrow Wilson, recalled his namesake from Mexico, and Huerta was isolated. Without supporters he could not retain control, and was shot dead in August, 1914. Carranza and Villa disputed the leadership of the country, while Zapata returned to the south. Carranza won the dispute, called a convention to discuss the future of Mexico. A constitution was drawn up and agreed to in January 1917.

The constitution was a revolutionary document which in some senses anticipated the Bolshevik Revolution of the same year. Three of its articles in particular will help us to understand the recent history of Mexico. First, Article 27 affirmed the right of the people to own the land and the minerals: by this article the law envisaged the return of the haciendas to the villages. Secondly, Article 123 recognised the right of the worker to organise, strike, and bargain collectively. An eight hour day, accident compensation and sick pay were promised. The clause affirmed that working for a living was to be considered a way of life, not simply an economic commodity subject to market changes of supply and demand. Thirdly, Article 3 excluded the Church from control of all levels of education, which was to be provided free at the elementary level.

Carranza was a northern landowner, and he did not approve the revolutionary doctrines embodied in the 1917 Constitution. His position at this time was fast becoming untenable. He was unable to establish order in many areas where followers of Zapata and Villa took no notice of orders from Mexico City. Meanwhile, Obregón, as yet a shadowy figure in the Revolution, began to organise support for himself. He was mainly responsible for the setting up of the official party of the Revolution, Partido Nacional Revolucionario (PNR), and he formed the urban workers into a trade union, CROM (Confederacíon Regional Obrera Mexicana). In 1920 he openly rebelled against Carranza, his former chief, who was conveniently murdered by one of his own officers. Obregón was declared President.

Obregon to Cárdenas (1920–1940)

The new President was not prepared to carry out the revolutionary programme in full. He was not keen to redistribute the land by wholesale seizures of haciendas, as Zapata demanded, and he left the initiative to the Indians themselves. As landowners were still able to use intimidation and force to resist expropriation, and Obregón was not prepared to risk their complete alienation, only a modest change of ownership took place. He was not prepared to allow Luis Morones, the leader of his trade union, CROM, to put pressures on employers to implement Article 123 of the Constitution. He did, however, encourage a vast educational building programme, designed to provide a school in every village. The curriculum was to consist of the Three Rs, the elements of agriculture and hygiene, and the doctrine of the Revolution.

In 1924 Obregón was succeeded as President by his own candidate, Plutarco Calles, who held power for ten years. Calles worked closely with Morones. They both made personal fortunes, and their radicalism became tempered by the fruits of office. After 1928 Calles resigned the presidency and ruled through a succession of pupper presidents, expecting to continue as the real power behind the scenes indefinitely. The PNR put forward a Six Year Plan to give renewed vigour to the efforts of Mexicans to implement the Constitution of 1917, and Calles accepted. He also accepted the Party's candidate, General Lázaro Cárdenas, as the next President, confident of his own ability to control the situation.

The Party's candidate was an exceptional man. He had known and served with the leading architects of the revolution during the decade of civil war, and he had proved himself an astute and wily politician under both Obregón and Calles. Most important of all, Cárdenas had a reputation for honesty and ability second to none in the Party, and a determination to implement the 1917 Constitution. He out-manoeuvred Calles and Morones, and crushed the last restive caudillos. He re-organised the PNR, to broaden its support. It was organised to represent the four sectors of Mexican society—military, labour, agrarian, and professional. A new trade union, called the CTM (Confederacíon de Trabajadores de Mexico), was established. It was purged of the influence of Morones, and followed a more radical policy.

A move to the left also marked Cárdenas' foreign policy. He actively supported Republican Spain and achieved popular acclaim by his expropriation of foreign oil companies in March 1938. Nationalism was the keynote of other aspects of his policy. In June 1937 he nationalised the railways, leaving the CTM responsible for operating them.

Cárdenas' greatest achievement, however, was undoubtedly his success in breaking up the haciendas, and redistributing the land. Eighteen million hectares changed hands during his six years in office, twice as much as had been changed between 1917 and 1934. Credit and machinery was also provided to help the new owners make effective use of their land. Cárdenas destroyed the hated hacienda system, replacing it with a self sufficient network of new ejidos, or communal farms. Finally, he intended to reinforce community life by making the school and not the Church the centre of village life. Cárdenas must surely rank as the greatest Mexican president of this century, for under his rule Mexico came nearer to achieving her revolutionary aims than under any other president.

Mexico since Cárdenas (1940–1971)

Five presidents have succeeded Cárdenas, and Mexico's unique political system continues to function very effectively. In 1945 the main party was renamed the Institutional Revolutionary Party, Partido de la Revolución Institucional (PRI), and has since lost its left wing image. It is now just as responsive to business and industrial interests as to those of the working classes. The opposition parties in Mexico have always contested elections and now they are promised minority representation in government.

In economic terms the last three decades have seen a change of emphasis from the agricultural to the industrial, but without the disastrous imbalance in the economy which resulted from such a move in Argentina. Land redistribution continues. Thirty-five million hectares have been added to the 65 million already redistributed by 1940, and approximately one-third of the country has been affected by agrarian reform arising from this policy. The success of this programme can best be shown by the fact that Mexico, with 45 million people, is virtually self sufficient in food-stuffs, whereas in 1910 £2·5 million a year was being spent on foodstuffs to help feed a population of under 15 million, out of a total import bill of £6 million. During the last twenty years over 20 million hectares have been brought into production through irrigation alone.

The change of emphasis, however, from agriculture to industry, has certainly taken place. Over half the gross national product comes from the manufacturing which employs 15% of the labour force. Industry is far more diversified than in any other Latin American country except Brazil, and Mexico has abundant mineral resources to provide its needs. Finally, the physical barriers to all types of development, provided by the geography of the land, are being overcome faster than in any other Latin American state.

By 1971 Mexico has established itself as one of the two leading states of Latin America, together with Brazil, but her political stability and continued economic expansion means that her development has been much more balanced. If we compare the two major exports of Brazil and Mexico this fact will become clear. Coffee and cotton provide over 60% of Brazil's exports, whereas for Mexico they constitute only 25%.

Mexico's progress from the Revolution has been the most encouraging indication in Latin America this century that massive social and economic problems can be overcome.

Chile: Alessandri's reforms (1920-1927)

The prosperity of Chile in 1914 was based on the extraction of nitrates from the Atacama Desert, and it gave her a false sense of well being. The old landowning families still held the reins of power, and resisted pressure to broaden the political system.

Events in Mexico and growing urban discontent led to the formation of a Liberal Alliance determined to change the traditional pattern of Chilean government. In 1920 the candidate of the Liberal Alliance, Arturo Alessandri, narrowly won the presidential election. Alessandri came from an immigrant family, and had lived in the northern mining province of Tarapacá. He symbolised the challenge to the hacendados of the Central Valley: he campaigned on a platform supporting the underprivileged, and he promised to break the political monopoly of the Central Valley. Once in power, however, Congress refused to pass Alessandri's reforms and in 1925 it was necessary for the army to intervene to break the dead-lock. Alessandri fled, but the junta which now ruled Chile recalled him to complete the work he had started. He introduced a new constitution to strengthen presidential powers and weaken Congress. Adult male suffrage was agreed upon, and a body of social reforms became law. Alessandri had successfully attacked the political power of the hacendados, though they still remained a powerful influence, and he had not replaced their influence.

Four years of progressive military dictatorship followed the end of Alessandri's presidency in 1927. The Depression years affected Chile as much as any other Latin American country. The currency devalued to one-sixth of its normal value, and for the first time for a century Chile defaulted on her debt payments. Between June and October 1932 there were nine governments, two general strikes, and a mutiny of the fleet. The Chilean economy collapsed.

Alessandri returned a second time as President from 1932 until 1938, and during this time restored the economic position, but he retained power by gaining conservative support, and his policies lost their radicalism. Any hope of replacing the hacendado class as the ruling group vanished, and like his Argentine contemporary, Irigoyen, Alessandri left a much needed social revolution unfinished.

The Popular Front and Radicals (1938-1952)

Though Alessandri was not prepared to carry out significant changes, the President elected in 1938, Pedro Aguirre Cerda, won power through support from a left wing coalition of working and middle class elements, a Popular Front government, which was anxious to see a fundamental change in the social and political structure take place. Cerda's government built schools and houses and developed industry. His three years in office have been described as 'the most energetic administration that Chile had enjoyed in the twentieth century'. Cerda's death in 1941 was particularly untimely since the radical party which dominated the presidency for the next ten years ceased to implement the necessary economic reforms and check the increasing size of the bureaucracy.

Christian democracy (1964-1970)

These problems remained unsolved when the Christian Democratic Party, led by Eduardo Frei, came to power in 1964. Three issues in particular needed urgent attention: first, the unbalanced economy, which was now heavily dependent on copper, just as it once had been on nitrates (70% of Chile's exports consist of copper); secondly, large ill-managed estates dominated Chile, and pressure for agrarian reform had increased. Chile is spending about £40 million a year on imported food. Thirdly, Chile's population has been growing at the rate of 2·4% a year, and pressure on her available land is greater than that on any of her neighbours—Chile can farm only 7% of its total area. Frei has had some success in dealing with the second and third problems. An agrarian reform bill became law in July 1967 and as a result of it Chile was expected to become self sufficient in foodstuffs within a few years. The economy has also been diversified. Heavy industry has developed in the area of Concepción, with the Huachipato steel works, and the coal reserves at Coronel. Santiago and Valparaiso both have thriving consumer goods industries. But Chile remains too vulnerable to the prices foreigners pay for its copper.

Frei's rise to power and reformist intentions threatened the power of the hacendados, but the Christian Democratic Party failed to withstand the opposition parties who united in Congress. In the 1970 elections support for the right-wing candidate was sufficiently strong to overthrow the Christian Democrats, and a Marxist president was elected by a small majority.

Uruguay (1903-1971)

By 1900 Uruguay had emerged from decades of foreign interference and internal squabbling, and made some progress towards economic prosperity. This progress continued until the Depression of 1929, and at the same time the country was transformed into the first welfare state in the Americas. The history of Uruguay in this period is the history of José Batlle y Ordóñez, twice President (from 1903 to 1907 and from 1911 to 1914), and the decisive influence in Uruguayan politics until his death in 1924. During his first presidency, Batlle defeated the last caudillo revolt, and allowed the press complete freedom. He set a new standard of honesty in elections by not attempting to perpetuate himself in office in 1907, and by not interfering with the choice of a successor. Before his return to power in 1911 he travelled in Europe, acquiring new ideas about government, and clarifying his own ideas about reform.

His second term (1911–1915) saw the creation of a welfare state. Free primary and secondary education was introduced. Workers were allowed the right to strike and organise unions, and were guaranteed an eight hour day, minimum wages, pensions and compensation for industrial injuries. Batlle anticipated much of the nationalist legislation introduced by both Vargas and Perón in the measures he adopted to control foreign capital. He believed in the power of the state to regulate and control public services, and he established a state mortgage and a state insurance bank in 1912. After the end of his second presidency his influence continued. In 1916 the Port of Montevideo was brought under state control. He set up public corporations to manage state monopolies, and during his lifetime they proved generally efficient and profitable.

Batlle also carried out constitutional reform. In 1916 he proposed the establishment of collegiate government on the Swiss model. This would have abolished the presidency, replacing it by a nine man National Council. Batlle had witnessed the rule of the caudillos in the nineteenth century, and he felt that the sharing of power within an elected National Council would prevent dictatorship. In fact, a compromise was evolved which allowed for both a President and a Council.

Batlle faced conservative opposition to his reforms, but the traditional conservative rallying point of the Roman Catholic Church had no strong influence. Divorce was legalised as early as

*The falls at Iguazú, Argentina, near the confluence
of the rivers Iguazú and Paraná*

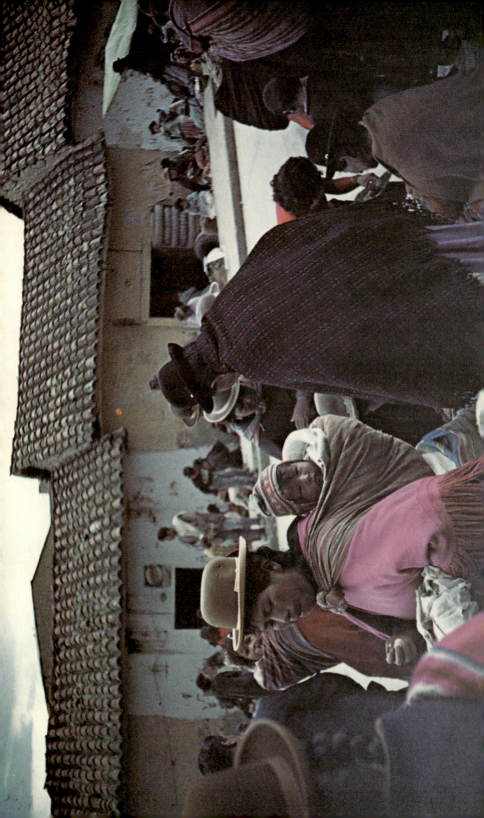

1907, and Uruguay became an officially atheist state under the constitution of 1917.

Politics since Batlle (1929-1971)

Batlle's death in 1929 coincided with the Depression, which threatened to undermine the social and economic benefits the working and middle classes then enjoyed. It also led to the rise to power of Gabriel Terra who ruled as a dictator from 1933 until 1938. Terra replaced Batlle's constitution of 1919 with his own, in which the executive consisted of one man, the president. Terra's firm decisive government certainly helped Uruguay to recover from the Depression.

For the next twenty years, the Colorado party to which Batlle had belonged continued in power until the Blancos at last won control. In 1951 collegiate government returned to Uruguay, but this time it was in the full sense that Batlle had intended in 1916, with no president. Since 1966, however, Uruguay has reverted to presidential rule.

The preoccupation of this small civilised country with constitutional problems seems to reflect the belief that the growing economic problems can be solved by manipulating the constitution. She depends for her livelihood on wool and meat exports, and these products have faced increasing competition. Batlle neglected agriculture, and the Colorados' preoccupation with the well-being of the capital, Montevideo, where 40% of the population live, is partly to blame for the mismanagement of the agricultural potential of the interior. But the Blancos have done little during their eight years (1958-1966) in office to redress the situation. Two other sectors of Uruguayan society also badly need reform. Industry is in urgent need of recapitalisation and economic incentive, while the civil service must reduce its manpower if the colossal burden the exchequer bears on its behalf is to be cut.

The activities of the urban guerillas, the Tupamaros, threaten the very existence of a free and democratic Uruguay. They have drawn attention to the economic and political weaknesses in Uruguayan society which neither Colorados nor Blancos have really faced.

Indians in the poorer suburbs of La Paz, Bolivia

Cuba (1898-1971)

Cuba is included in this first group of six Latin American countries because as a Spanish colony she had a strong economy; and after the war of 1898 her dependence on Spain was replaced by a close relationship with the United States. In the last ten years, Cuba has made a determined effort to break away from her economic dependence on North America.

Cuba emerged from colonialism with the help of the United States. In 1898 the United States Congress declared that 'the people of the island of Cuba are, and of right ought to be, free and independent'. Congress demanded Spain's withdrawal from the island and authorised President McKinley to use force against the mother country if necessary. In the war that followed Spain was defeated, and by the peace treaty the United States assumed responsibility for the establishment of a viable, independent Cuban government. The next two and a half years saw an improvement in living standards as a result of the recovery of the Cuban economy, the eradication of yellow fever, and the establishment of an educational system. In May 1902 the interim military government handed over power to an independently elected Cuban government.

But the United States Congress, despite its earlier statement, was determined that Cuba should be a subservient neighbour and stipulated than an amendment should be written into the Cuban constitution. Under Article 3 of the constitution

> Cuba consents that the United States may exercise the right to intervene for the preservation of Cuban independence, the maintenance of a government adequate for the protection of life, property, and individual liberty.

For thirty-two years Cuba's constitution contained this clause known as the Platt Amendment, and it affected her independent existence. But the position was advantageous to Cuba in that the United States supported her economy. In 1903, the year following the establishment of the elected Cuban government, the two countries signed a preferential tariff agreement which gave Cuban sugar exports special terms. The Platt Amendment remained part of the Cuban constitution until 1934, and during the years before it was abrogated the United States intervened to preserve political stability, first between 1906 and 1909, and then in 1917. She also supervised elections in an effort to establish democracy, but her efforts were to no avail. In these circumstances anti-American feeling grew in Cuba. In 1933 a young sergeant, Fulgencio Batista, led a group of non-commissioned officers in a revolt to overthrow the pro-American dictator, General Machado.

Batista had originally been supported by anti-American elements who favoured nationalist policies, but once in power he clearly identified himself with United States business interests. In 1952 Batista tried to reinforce his position by assuming even greater powers, and this action prompted a revolt on July 26th, 1953 at the Moncada Barracks in Santiago. The leader of the revolt, a young lawyer named Fidel Castro, was captured and jailed, but released in 1954 and allowed to go to Mexico. In December 1956 he returned to Cuba, survived Batista's attempt to destroy his small band of followers, and from his refuge in the Sierra Madre mountains, he planned the dictator's overthrow. His seizure of power on January 1st, 1959 was to a great extent due to Batista's loss of popular and middle class support and his regime's close alliance with United States business interests.

Fidel Castro (1959–1971)

Castro's aims were at first simply the restoration of democracy, economic nationalism and social justice, but in 1959 it became apparent that his plans were more far reaching. With some modifications his policy has moved steadily towards the left, and his regime has now become a ruthless dictatorship.

Castro's first moves to establish a left wing state were the expropriation of foreign companies, and so far he has brought 90% of industry under state control. Large estates have been broken up and the land redistributed to the peasants. A mass education programme was started which aimed to eliminate illiteracy, and was also a means of political indoctrination. Cuban trade was reorientated away from the United States towards Eastern Europe. The production of sugar was at first reduced because of its earlier

Fidel Castro enters Havana, 1st January 1959.

associations with the imperialist United States, and also because
the economy needed diversification. These efforts bear a close
resemblance to events in the Mexican Revolution.

The United States feared the establishment of a communist
dominated state ninety kilometres from Florida, and in April
1961 she supported an invasion by anti-Castro Cubans which
convinced Castro that the United States intended to take over the
island and force him out of power. Ties with the USSR were
strengthened and Castro publicly declared that he had always been
a Marxist-Leninist. The revolutionary movement became dominated by communists. The Russians established a missile site in
Cuba, and the United States intelligence service obtained photographs of their presence. In October 1962 President Kennedy
challenged the Russians to withdraw their rockets from Cuba or
face an attack on their ships supplying Cuba. The Russians backed
down and the crisis ended.

Its effects were twofold. In the first place Castro became more
and more disenchanted with the USSR, which he felt had let him
down. Some of his advisers, especially 'Che' Guevara, encouraged
the idea of fomenting world revolution and moving away from
Moscow's cautious foreign policy; but Guevara's attempts to
'export' revolution had failed even before his death in 1967 in
Bolivia. The present state of Cuba's relations with the USSR is
difficult to surmise because Castro's disenchantment since the

'missile' crisis, has not blinded him to the economic necessity of keeping on friendly terms with her. The second effect of the Cuban crisis was that Latin American governments, who had first seen the Cuban Revolution as a victory for progress, demanded action against Castro. In 1964 all the OAS (Organisation of American States) member states, except Mexico, broke off diplomatic relations with Cuba.

It is difficult to draw up a balance sheet of the unfinished Cuban Revolution. The success in creating more educational opportunities and building more schools is recognised. The last few years have witnessed a cultural revolution which still remains remarkably free from political control. Agrarian reform has also been achieved. But neither the efforts to diversify agriculture, nor the introduction of heavy industry, have succeeded. Castro, in a speech in July 1970, in fact accepted responsibility for the economic failures of his regime. The basic necessities of life are more fairly distributed in Cuba today, but there are shortages of almost every commodity. The promised democracy does not exist, but Castro remains a popular dictator, unlikely to be overthrown.

The Cuban Revolution is best understood as part of the challenge to the old order, embodied in this case by the alliance of the United States business interests and the Cuban upper and middle classes under Batista. It has been a revolution which has owed much to the experiences of Mexico half a century earlier.

There are both threads of continuity and change in the stories of the six most advanced states this century. The challenge to the traditional governing classes in four countries came from middle class urban groups. Irigoyen, Alessandri and Batlle were all leaders of the middle class. Perón and Vargas broadened their appeal by gaining some military support, but also by using the urban working classes as a counter to any reaction. 'Peronismo' and 'Getúlismo' are both potent forces in Argentina and Brazil today. In Mexico the challenge was more complex because the revolution revived the conflict between Indians and creoles which had existed at the Conquest, at the time of emancipation, and during the period of Juárez's rule. In Cuba the revolution followed a predictable pattern, but owed much of its development to the special relationship of the United States with the island.

Bolivia

Two other revolutions in Latin America have left their mark on the continent since World War II, those of Bolivia and Guatemala. In Bolivia the national revolution began in 1952. It was an attempt to make the country industrially and agriculturally self-sufficient. Like that of Mexico it has been a revolution in which the Indians demanded their lands, lost at the time of the Conquest. It has also followed the pattern of Latin American revolutions by leading to a takeover by the government of private enterprises, in this case the tin mines.

The claim has been made by Professor Alexander that the Bolivian Revolution was the most profound social change in Latin America since the Mexican Revolution. It was put forward in 1957 after only five years of revolution, but now it seems a doubtful claim. The majority of Indians have not been integrated into society. The original leaders of the revolution, Paz Estenssoro, Juan Lechín and Siles Zuaso, are in exile. The tin mines have become less productive than before state ownership. Within the last four years Bolivia has recovered somewhat; it could not be claimed that the economy is viable, but certainly there is evidence that some stability has been achieved. The agricultural potential of the tropical eastern part of the country can now be helped by the building of better communications to the Altiplano. Santa Cruz has all the appearance of a boom town since oil was developed. Bolivia receives constant grants from the United States and will only become self reliant after decades of stable government. The traveller in Bolivia is always amazed that so much progress has been made because the land is still the most divided in Latin America.

Guatemala

Guatemala's revolution of 1944 followed fourteen years of oppressive fascist style dictatorship under General Jorge Ubico. It followed the pattern of the Mexican revolution. Reformers demanded a redistribution of wealth, greater educational opportunities and facilities, and the implementation of agrarian reform. The first President after the revolution, Juan Arevalo (1945-1951) and his successor, Jacobo Arbenz (1951-1954), sought greater economic independence for Guatemala. The main objects of attack were the United States business interests which dominated the country. President Truman's administration objected to the refusal of the Guatemalan government to repress communist elements, and resented the pressure placed on business concerns like the United Fruit Company.

In 1952 Arbenz had passed an agrarian reform bill and in two years expropriated 600,000 hectares of land from the company. This land, together with 200,000 hectares of additional land, was reallocated to 100,000 peasants. In 1954 the United States obtained a majority vote at the Inter-American Conference at Caracas condemning the 'domination or control of the political institutions of any American state by the International Communist Movement' and Arbenz was overthrown. An army colonel, Castillo Armas, was made Head of State, supported by the Roman Catholic Church and the traditional ruling classes.

The Guatemalan Revolution ended after ten years, following the foreign intervention on behalf of anti-communist forces. Land was returned to its former owners, the United Fruit Company recovered much of its property, and Guatemala has reverted to its pre-revolutionary state. Arbenz had become a tool of communist forces, and some of his attempts to implement land collectivisation in tropical America on a Russian pattern were unrealistic, but it will be difficult to prevent social and economic changes taking place in the future, and under a dictatorship these are likely to be violent. The best hope for peaceful change lies with the Central American Common Market, which has so far been remarkably successful in bringing economic stability to the Central American countries.

United States policy in Latin America

The United States exercises great influence in Latin America, especially in the Caribbean region. Arbenz lost power in Guatemala because the United States decided not to tolerate his revolution any longer. Cuba's relationship with the world has been governed by her emotional reaction to United States control of her economy over many years. Yet the North American giant who has been so often caricatured in Latin America as an ogre, a black Caliban, has done more to develop the countries to the south of the Rio Grande than any other nation this century. The United States has also changed its political attitude towards Latin American countries. In the 1930s President F. D. Roosevelt adopted the 'Good Neighbour' policy, changing the traditional role which the United States had played by treating Latin American countries as equal. In 1934 he abrogated the Platt Amendment, and in 1938 he would not support a strong line demanded by United States business interests threatened with the expropriation of their holdings in Mexico. In 1961 President Kennedy continued this policy by launching the 'Alliance for Progress' programme which was almost a Marshall Aid plan for Latin America. Both these Presidents showed a rare understanding of the Latin American outlook, but to this day many North American politicians remain preoccupied with the spectre of communism.

Latin America faces many problems that will only be solved with the political and economic understanding of the North Americans. The twentieth century developments in the other twelve republics illustrate this fact time and time again.

Haiti

The two states of Haiti and the Dominican Republic have both been controlled by the United States this century. Between 1915 and 1934 United States marines ruled Haiti, and between 1916 and 1924 they controlled the Dominican Republic. United States rule in both countries followed and was succeeded by chaos and dictatorship. In Haiti the spirit of François Duvalier, 'Papa Doc', still survives. The country is the poorest in Latin America, and has the most tyrannical dictatorship. The average income of Haitians is about £25 per head each year, and population density is the highest in Latin America.

Dominican Republic

The Dominican Republic experienced an equally ruthless dictatorship under Trujillo from 1930 to 1961, but unlike Duvalier his rule did bring a few material benefits to his country at the price of tyranny. The country's prosperity has since been undermined by political instability. After the assassination of Trujillo, Juan Bosch became in February 1963 the first constitutionally elected President since 1924. He was unseated by the military in September 1963, who retained control until May 1965, when United States intervention put an end to the raging civil war, but not to political instability. Anti-American feelings are still strong: in March 1970 a United States military attaché was held to ransom for days, until left-wing political prisoners were released.

A familiar economic situation exists in the Dominican Republic, common to many of the Latin American republics. Measures to diversify the economy and deal with chronic problems of unemployment and poverty cannot be effective until political stability is achieved, while at the same time unless economic progress is made, political instability will remain.

Central America

In recent years the five Central American Republics have made economic progress. They cannot be regarded simply as 'Banana Republics' (an abusive description made of many Latin American states, especially the Central American Republics in the ninteenth century). The reasons for prosperity have been the initial success of the Central American Common Market. It was set up in 1961 to bring about the development of a free trade area in which five countries, Guatemala, Salvador, Honduras, Nicaragua and Costa Rica would participate. The CACM was highly successful during its first five years. Trade within the region rose from 50 million dollars in 1962 to 176 million dollars within three years, while external trade also expanded. El Salvador increased its exports by over 50% between 1960 and 1965. The increase in production of Honduras has outstripped the increase in population, and she has managed to control inflation. The progress of Nicaragua during the ten year period (1953-1963) was even more spectacular. The cost of living has remained at a very low level, while national production increased by 75%, and per capita income from 226 dollars per head to 292 dollars per head.

The left-wing revolution in Guatemala helped to focus attention on Central America, and break down ignorance of the area. She herself, despite the legacy of this frustrated revolution, has been expanding at the rate of 5% a year since the establishment of CACM.

The fifth member of the free trade area, Costa Rica, has never fitted conveniently into generalisations about Central America. She was a democracy when the other states were ruled by caudillos. She was a land settled by Europeans who formed the majority, unlike mestizo Honduras, Nicaragua and El Salvador, or Indian Guatemala. But she was, like her neighbours, dependent on two crops, bananas and coffee, for her livelihood. The Central American Common Market has been least beneficial to Costa Rica because her economic standards were already well above those of the area. She remains a haven of democracy in a politically unsettled area. The degree of political stability that exists in Costa Rica can best be gauged by two statements. Only twice this century, from 1917 to 1918, and in 1948, has a democratic form of government been replaced by dictatorship. In 1948, when civilian rule was restored, the army was disbanded and declared illegal.

Panama

The last republic in Latin America to gain independence was Panama. It has existed for only sixty-seven years as an independent state, and its history has been closely involved with that of the Panama Canal.

Ferdinand de Lesseps, the successful builder of the Suez Canal, spent ten years trying to build a sea level canal in Panama without using locks. In 1884 his scheme collapsed, resulting in a financial scandal which shook France. The United States government took up the idea of building a canal there, and the Spanish American War of 1898 dramatically illustrated the value of controlling the isthmus. In 1902 President Theodore Roosevelt was authorised to buy out the French company, and make a treaty with Colombia for the building of the canal. The Colombian Senate delayed signing the treaty, and Panamanians appealed to the United States for support in a war of independence against Colombia.

The United States government was exasperated by Colombia's procrastination, but gave no promise of aid. The Panamanian separatists nevertheless believed that a definite promise had been made, and the revolution broke out. Within hours the United States warship *S. S. Nashville* appeared at Colon, and two days later Panama's independence was recognised by the United States. A treaty was signed between the two countries, based on the proposed treaty of alliance between Colombia and the United States. It gave the United States sovereignty over a strip of land which measured sixteen kilometres wide across the eighty kilometres of the isthmus. The canal was built and completed within this area in 1914.

Panama depends on the Canal Zone for its revenue, and this again underlines the importance of the United States in Latin America. The Panamanians dislike the continued foreign control of the canal, and there are periodic riots to demonstrate their feeling. At present the treaty between the United States and Panama is being re-negotiated to make it more acceptable to national feeling. But without the United States presence the prosperity of Panama would have scarcely reached the level it has, for there has been little political stability. Between 1903 and 1967 there have been forty-seven presidents, of whom only three completed their terms of office.

The five states that remain to be considered are all in South America. Their histories illustrate the variety of South America, and the theme of this chapter, which is the challenge to the old order. Colombia, Venezuela and Peru are all examples of states experiencing the social and economic changes that affected the ABC states earlier this century. Ecuador has made sporadic advances economically, but without gaining very much over the long term. Paraguay remains an unrelenting dictatorship controlled by President Stroessner.

Venezuela

In terms of material change Venezuela has made the greatest progress of these five states. In the nineteenth century Guzmán Blanco brought some stability at the price of setting a disastrous example of venality and corruption to his successors. In 1914 Venezuela was a backward nation even by Latin American standards. Her chief exports were coffee and cacao and her total trade was in fact less than that of Bolivia, and only slightly above that of the Dominican Republic. After World War I, Venezuela began exporting oil, and by 1930 she was producing 10% of the world's supply. Juan Gómez, dictator from 1908-1935, used the money to pay off the country's debts, increase urban development, and spread industrialisation. Caracas grew in size from a city of 200,000 people to one of over 2 million, in twenty-five years. Today Venezuela depends on oil. It accounts for 70% of the national revenue, 90% of exports, and over 80% of foreign investment.

The transformation of Venezuela's cities contrasts with the backwardness of the countryside, where standards are still very low. In 1964 the United Nations estimated the average income of Venezuelans at almost eight hundred dollars per head, which is the highest in Latin America and compares favourably with many European countries. But the average income of the peasant families, which form the greatest part of the population, is perhaps one-quarter of that figure. Venezuela, more than any other state, illustrates the contrasts of Latin America: the opulence of the centre of Caracas, and its ramshackle poor quarters; the landed estates, and the landless peasants; and a heavy dependence on one commodity, oil, of which there is now a world surplus.

It is only within the last ten years that a sustained attempt has been made to correct the glaring imbalance of Venezuelan life. Two Presidents, Romúlo Betancourt (1959-1964), and Rául Leoni (1964-1969), have established a democratic form of government after a weary succession of dictatorships, and despite terrorism inspired from Cuba. Land reform has begun: so far about one-quarter of the peasant families have received plots of land. Industry has been diversified by developing part of the Orinoco Basin for an iron and steel industry. In recent years the rich province of Guyana has also been developed, since the River Orinoco has been bridged.

Colombia

Venezuela remains relatively untouched by social reform and one cannot speak of a social revolution, even on the limited scale that Chile has carried out. Colombia's experience has been similar. She began the twentieth century by counting the cost of her bloody civil war in 1898-1902, and by losing Panama in 1903. There could be no illusions about the country's weakness and yet democratic governments succeeded each other at regular intervals. There was political stability because the two traditional parties, Conservatives and Liberals, respected free elections. But the economy was heavily dependent on coffee, and could not survive the slump in world prices in the 1920s. Democratic government continued to survive during the Depression years, but familiar conservative policies were adopted: nationalist reforms were instituted, and protective tariffs built up. Within this framework the social structure of the country remained unaltered.

In the last twenty years change has taken place. The majority of Colombians now live in cities—Bogotá has a population of 2 million, and Medellín and Cali each well over 500,000. The economy has been diversified. Oil products now rank second to coffee as a foreign currency earner; a strong textile industry has been established at Medellín and Cali. Social change and constructive reform of the traditional bastions of conservatism, the Church and the army, might then have been expected to follow, but instead violence erupted. Between 1948 and 1957, 200,000 people died while the politicians feuded. A strong dictator, Rojas Pinilla, took power until Conservatives and Liberals at last realised the senselessness of violence. Since 1957 the two parties have agreed to alternate in office and this has succeeded in restoring Colombia's reputation as a democratic state. But neither party has brought about the fundamental social changes which are necessary if violence is to be avoided in a land where left wing guerilla movements are well established.

Ecuador

The problems which face Colombia and Venezuela can be overcome if they maintain political stability, and can spread the benefits of increased efficiency to the poorest groups. Ecuador's future cannot be seen in the same optimistic light.

Half her population is Indian. She is heavily dependent on two exports, bananas and cacao. She has no mineral resources like her northern neighbours, and the Andes split the country into two quite separate regions: the coastal lowlands around Guayaquil, and the mountain area surrounding Quito, 3,000 metres up in the Andes. In Colombia and Venezuela communications have helped to bridge physical divisions, but in Ecuador the railway between Quito and Guayaquil has not united the two regions, but only served to under-line their separateness. In recent years the birthrate has been increasing at the rate of 3·3% a year. Agricultural production must be increased; and in the lowlands some progress has taken place, but the conservatism of Andean landowners and the Indians has prevented the proper use of land in the highlands.

Paraguay

There are many similarities between Ecuador and Paraguay. They are both dependent on agricultural products for their foreign currency. They have been ruled more often by military dictators than by constitutionally elected civilians, though Ecuador has had some democratically elected presidents since the war (between 1948 and 1961, and between 1966 and 1970). They both support large Indian and mestizo populations. Perhaps the most important similarity between them is that they are both divided lands.

Paraguay west of the River Paraguay is called the Chaco. It covers over half the country's area and it was the scene of the Chaco War (1932-1935) in which Paraguay recovered her national prestige, which she had lost in the War of the Triple Alliance (1865-1870), by defeating Bolivia. The futility of such a war, which only satisfied wounded national pride, can be illustrated by the fact that only 50,000 people live in the Chaco, a vast area of scrubland which covers 247,085 square kilometres. The east bank of the River Paraguay makes up the other 159,665 square kilometres of the country, and has 2 million people. The Chaco has been of no commercial value to the Paraguayans, and the Chaco War simply reinforced militarism. It came at a time when Paraguay was recovering from the effects of the War of the Triple Alliance, and it has clearly delayed economic progress in Paraguay.

The Paraguayans have an average income of about £45 each per annum, the lowest in South America, and second only to Haiti in all Latin America. Her agriculture is still at subsistence level, over half the production being mandioc. Paraguay has no direct links to the sea, and is, like Bolivia, dependent on the goodwill of neighbours for her trade. Argentina controls about 40% of her trade, and as many as 300,000 Paraguayans work and live there.

The present ruler, Alfredo Stroessner (1954-   ) has done little to improve conditions in Paraguay except provide political stability. Asunción seems little more than a sleepy provincial town in comparison with most capitals in Latin America, though it symbolises the charm of an isolated, if beautiful, land. It is difficult to visualise how Paraguay will ever be more than a backwater.

Peru

The history of Peru in this century has been as turbulent as in the nineteenth century. Her defeat by Chile in the War of the Pacific (1879-1883), and the economic decline which set in with the fall in demand for guano, led to internal disquiet. The traditional ruling classes squabbled for power, oblivious of the wretched state in which both Indian and mestizo lived. Nicolás de Pierola, the founder of the Democratic Party, was the first President to begin the process of modernisation.

By 1914 education had been developed, and agricultural methods on the coastal estates brought up to date. The dictatorship of Augusto Leguía (1919-1930) also fostered material progress, but prosperity was based on foreign investors, especially North American mining interests. Between 1919 and 1928 Peru's foreign debts rose tenfold from 10 million dollars, and the world Depression completely undermined the economy.

CHAPTER SEVEN

Leguía's chief rival was Raúl Haya de la Torre who in 1924 founded APRA (Alianza Popular Revolucionaria Americana), a radical party which attacked foreign imperialism, supported the Indians, and wanted to establish a socialist style economy. Haya de la Torre's movement was the first in any Andean country which specifically aimed to bring the Indians into the political and economic life of the state. It obviously threatened the traditional power structure, and not surprisingly APRA was kept out of power by the creole oligarchy. In 1945 the ruling class decided to offer Haya de la Torre a share in the government of José Bustamente, but he feared that it might compromise his revolutionary ideals. Instability between 1945 and 1948 led to a seizure of power by the dictator Manuel Odría. He was not able to sustain the prosperity which resulted from a boom in the price of metals during the Korean War (1950-1953), and as prices tumbled the government resorted to printing paper money, and Peru found herself in yet another inflationary situation.

Peru's recent progress has been remarkable if one remembers the strained economy of the early 1950s. She has sustained a growth rate of about 5% for a decade, and during those years become the world's leading fishing nation. The number of fish meal factories (the main buyers of fish) increased in Peru from twenty-seven in 1956 to one hundred and ten in 1962. Mining has also expanded, Peru being among the largest producers of copper, lead and zinc in the world. But alongside this encouraging picture must be set the obstacles to progress and change. Population is increasing at over 3% per annum, and food production has not kept pace with this growth. The drift from the countryside to the towns has increased until over half of Peru's 12 million people live in urban areas. The agricultural sector of the economy is losing manpower at a time when more intensive cultivation of the land is essential. On the Altiplano alone 1,233 landowners own 80% of the total usable arable and pastoral land, while hundreds of thousands of tiny plots, too small to be efficiently worked, need urgent amalgamation.

In 1962 the veteran APRA leader, Haya de la Torre, won the presidential election. But once in power he showed little interest in reform. He was prepared to collaborate with the former dictator, President Odría, in order to hold on to power. The army refused to accept the election result and in 1963 new elections took place. The conservative Fernando Beláunde was elected. Real hope for change survived under Beláunde's energetic administration. Whereas Haya de la Torre had become the seeker after office at all costs, Beláunde set out to see for himself the real nature of Peru's problems. He may be added to the list of post-war leaders in Latin America, like Frei in Chile, Betancourt in Venezuela, and Lleras Camargo in Colombia, who were prepared to carry out social and economic changes to forestall the possibilities of Cuba style revolutions, leading to dictatorship. Beláunde faced as difficult a task as any head of state to achieve a revolution through democracy, and he was deposed by a military coup led by General Velasco in October, 1968.

Conclusion

Within the last century various attempts to bring about a change have been made in Latin America. Success has eluded all countries with the possible exception of Mexico, where popular governments have maintained and increased a remarkable rate of expansion since the war. Mexico's rate of growth since 1940 has been maintained at 7%, a unique achievement in the world. Three states, Guatemala (1944), Bolivia (1952), and Cuba (1959) have tried to follow Mexico's revolutionary example, but they have not so far succeeded.

The ABC states followed Uruguay's early example (1903), and became democratic, but either popular dictators took control and failed to check inflation, as in Brazil and Argentina, or lack of leadership undermined economies which were very vulnerable to world price fluctuation, as in Chile and Uruguay.

Within the last decade the Andean republics and Central American states have at last begun to break free from dictatorship and economic stagnation. Only Haiti, perhaps the most brutal dictatorship in the world, and Paraguay, traditionalist and slow moving, remain untouched by the challenge to the old order.

CHAPTER EIGHT

Three problems facing Latin America

The progress of Latin American states in the future will depend on their ability to deal with the three problems raised in the opening chapter: how to feed the growing population and at the same time control a further explosion of the population; how to spread and improve educational facilities; and how to develop the national economies of the twenty republics in order to make them more viable and less dependent on fluctuations in the world prices for primary products.

One country, Mexico, stands out as an example of what can be achieved in the face of these great obstacles. It has devised a political system which has provided stable conditions allowing for the growth of the per capita income, which has more than kept pace with a birthrate increase of 3·2%. Illiteracy is gradually being eliminated: by 1960 it had been reduced to 35% of the population of fifteen years of age and over. The economy is diversified; export figures are higher than imports. Mexico has one commercial advantage: it is earning £100 million a year from tourists, and this ensures that the balance of payments figures remain good.

Population explosion

Other countries have not so far succeeded in matching Mexico's achievement. Latin America's population is increasing at the staggering rate of 50 million every seven years. In the decade 1950-1960 it grew by 2·7% per annum, compared with Africa's 2·1% and Asia's 1·8% growth rates. Between 1961 and 1968 Latin America's growth rate increased to 3·1%. The population figures since 1900 make startling reading:

> 1900—61 million
> 1934—111 million
> 1967—250 million
> 2000—estimated 550 million

Population Tables

	(in millions)		PROJEC-TIONS	% RACIAL COMPOSITION OF POPULATION			
	1960	1968	1980	white	mestizo	indian	negroid
ARGENTINA	20.85	23.62	27.58	89	9	2	
BOLIVIA	3.82	4.68	5.97	12	31	57	
BRAZIL	69.73	88.21	123.57	39	20	3	37
CHILE	7.68	9.35	12.91	25	66	9	
COLOMBIA	15.40	19.82	28.29	20	59	12	9
COSTA RICA	1.25	1.63	2.73	48	47	2	3
CUBA	6.82	8.07	10.07	30	20		49
DOMINICAN R.	3.04	4.03	6.17	5	14		81
ECUADOR	4.36	5.70	8.47	7	32	58	3
EL SALVADOR	2.45	3.27	4.91	8	52	40	
GUATEMALA	3.81	4.86	7.19	3	30	67	
HAITI	3.99	4.70	6.92				100
HONDURAS	1.85	2.41	3.77	10	45	40	5
MEXICO	36.05	47.27	72.39	9	61	29	1
NICARAGUA	1.41	1.91	2.82	10	77	4	9
PANAMA	1.06	1.37	1.99	8	50	10	31
PARAGUAY	1.75	2.23	3.36	5	30	65	
PERU	10.02	12.77	18.53	13	37	49	1
URUGUAY	2.54	2.82	3.25	90	8		2
VENEZUELA	7.35	9.69	14.49	12	68	10	10
TOTAL	205.23	258.41	365.38				

The mortality rate has declined equally dramatically, falling by over 50% in Costa Rica between 1935 and 1958, and everywhere else by at least 25% over the same period. Improved medical techniques are therefore largely responsible for the rapid increases in population. In 1964 President Lopez Mateos of Mexico, in his farewell speech to Congress, said that during his presidency (1958–1964) the average life expectancy of a Mexican had increased from fifty-two years to sixty-four years.

The population explosion has not been matched by economic expansion. Even where increases in population have been lowest, as in Argentina (1·7% between 1947 and 1965) and Uruguay (1·1% between 1945 and 1965), annual rates of growth in real income have been as low, or even lower. Countries such as Venezuela, Peru and the five Central American Republics, which have recently enjoyed a decade of economic expansion, have been faced with population increases of over 3·0% per annum. Inflation has in many cases ensured that any benefits of increased prosperity which still remain have been cancelled.

The total picture is depressing. Between 1963 and 1968 population in Latin America increased by 12%, and food production by 10%. The problem is made worse by depopulation of the rural areas and the consequent loss of farm labour. Food is becoming more expensive as the migration to the urban areas continues. The pressure on the urban areas is mounting so rapidly that the public services are breaking down, and there are large areas of appalling slums in all the principle cities. Ten per cent of the region's people live in four great cities: Buenos Aires, Mexico City, Río de Janeiro and São Paulo, which have 22 million people in total. Unemployment and under employment are serious problems, in these cities.

Education

Education is generally recognised to be the remedy for the problems of developing countries, and the Latin American countries are no exception. Literacy figures do provide a guide to the relative standards of education in different countries, and in Latin America the figures for Argentina, Chile and Uruguay are the most advanced. Their literacy rates and their figures of school enrolment bear comparison with a Western European country like Italy. At the other end of the scale, six states had over 60% of their population over fifteen years of age illiterate in 1950: Haiti (89%), Guatemala (71%), Bolivia (68%), Honduras (65%), Nicaragua (62%), and El Salvador (61%). There has been an improvement in the last twenty years, but since figures tend to underestimate the problem, those mentioned above still serve as a reasonably accurate guide today.

In the decade 1950–1960, figures for the Latin American countries show that school enrolments at all levels increased—at the primary level by 5%, at the secondary level by 10%, and higher education by 8%. Governments also spent more on education. Peru, Mexico, Bolivia, Venezuela, Costa Rica, Panama and Cuba are all spending between 24% and 27% of the national budget each

Education and Cost of Living Tables

EDUCATION	COST OF LIVING
A % ILLITERATE AT 15 B % OF 5-14s ENROLLED (1950) C NOS. IN HIGHER EDUCATION per 1000	BASE = 100 (1963) A ALL ITEMS B FOOD

LATIN AMERICA	A	B	C	A	B	OTHER COUNTRIES	A	B
ARGENTINA	9	66	4.8	311	304	United Kingdom	121	118
BOLIVIA	68	24	1.7	142	144	United States	114	114
BRAZIL	39	26	1.0	714	650	West Germany	113	108
CHILE	16	66	2.9	346	343	Japan	127	131
COLOMBIA	38	28	0.9	167	164	Spain	144	138
COSTA RICA	16	49		108	111	Ghana	154	157
CUBA	22	49	1.9			Indonesia	57,712	62,876
DOMINICAN R.	36	40	1.1	102	104			
ECUADOR	33	41	1.3	113	119			
EL SALVADOR	52	31	0.6	105	109			
GUATEMALA	62	22	0.8	102	103			
HAITI	89	15	0.3	119	118			
HONDURAS	55	22	0.6	115	112			
MEXICO	35	39	1.1	116	118			
NICARAGUA	50	23	0.8	113	122			
PANAMA	23	54	1.9	106	110			
PARAGUAY	26	51	1.2	109	106			
PERU	40	44	1.9	131	130			
URUGUAY	10	62	4.8	1,649	1,768			
VENEZUELA	34	40	1.4	107	103			

year. Elsewhere the level of investment in education is lower, but all states except Guatemala do spend at least one-tenth of their total revenue on education.

The existing educational facilities are not being used enough, however, and the student wastage rate is very high. In Latin America only three students out of every hundred complete

CHAPTER EIGHT

secondary schooling, while only one in every thousand finishes a course he started at university or college. In Brazil and Venezuela only 0·03% and 0·06% respectively of students complete their higher educational courses, while even in Uruguay and Argentina only 0·7% succeed. Teaching methods tend to be old fashioned and dreary. The report of the third inter-American meeting of education ministers (1963) pointed out some of the defects of existing secondary education:

> learning by rote, absence of student orientation and guidance services, predominance of rigid undifferentiated, uncorrelated and encyclopaedic curricula. . . .

It went on to criticise the lack of pupil participation in lessons, the inadequacy of intelligence testing, and the defectiveness of most textbooks and equipment. The distinguished Argentine economist, Dr Rául Prebisch said in 1962 that there was:

> a need for real revolution in the educational systems, not only in the educational process itself but also in finding solutions to the serious financial difficulties which prevent gifted men from rising to higher fields.

The quality of education is often poor at the higher education level. There are one hundred and thirty-two universities in Latin America, whose standards vary enormously. They have an enrolment of over 500,000 students. Most of them are not universities in the British sense, only offering courses of lectures which train the student to pass examinations to qualify for the professions like engineering, medicine and law. Opportunities to study arts or science subjects for their own sake, as an academic discipline, rarely exist. The student of history, for instance, could only study that subject as part of a course to become a teacher.

Latin America needs skilled leaders who are more than trained professional men, who are able to understand the need for reforms, and who have the practical ability to carry them out. Most writers are hopeful that Dr Prebisch's 'real revolution' will be achieved. To quote one recent commentator, William Benton:

> If there is any key to the future that is most helpful, it is education.

Trade Tables

VALUES IN MILLIONS OF U.S. DOLLARS

	1 IMPORTS		2 EXPORTS		3 MAJOR EXPORTS	
					TOTAL	INDIVIDUAL
	1960	1968	1960	1968	1967	1967

LATIN AMERICA

	1960	1968	1960	1968	1967	1967
ARGENTINA	1,249	1,149	1,077	1,374	1,464	MEAT 382 WHEAT 137 CORN 223
BOLIVIA	69	151	51	164	166	TIN 91
BRAZIL	1,462	1,856	1,269	1,881	1,654	COFFEE 705 COTTON 91 IRON ORE 103
CHILE	562	868	488	915	910	COFFEE 712 IRON ORE 78
COLOMBIA	519	601	466	520	510	COFFEE 322 PETROLEUM 61
COSTA RICA	110	191	86	172	144	COFFEE 55 BANANAS 31
DOMINICAN R.	100	217	174	163	156	SUGAR 90
ECUADOR	114	191	144	210	200	BANANAS 125 (estimate)
EL SALVADOR	122	218	117	212	208	COFFEE 100 COTTON 30
GUATEMALA	138	247	117	200	199	COFFEE 68 COTTON 32
HAITI	36	40	33	36	33	COFFEE 14
HONDURAS	72	171	63	184	156	BANANAS 78
MEXICO	1,186	1,969	764	1,254	1,145	COTTON 143 SUGAR 82 COFFEE 60 SHRIMP 59
NICARAGUA	72	165	56	159	146	COTTON 56 COFFEE 21
PANAMA	128	274	27	95	92	BANANAS 49 PETROLEUM 23 (REFINED)
PARAGUAY	38	71	27	47	48	MEAT 17 TIMBER 8
PERU	373	663	430	846	774	COPPER 230 FISHMEAL 197
URUGUAY	218	162	129	179	159	WOOL 79 MEAT 40
VENEZUELA	1,188	1,448	2,432	2,886	2,886	PETROLEUM 2665

WORLD TRADE

World total	132,766	225,100	126,572	212,600	excl. CUBA, SOVIET BLOC & mainland CHINA
United Kingdom	13,033	18,959	10,611	15,346	
United States	16,375	36,012	20,601	34,660	
West Germany	10,107	20,235	11,418	24,854	
Japan	4,491	12,988	4,055	12,973	
Latin America	7,720	11,600	7,950	11,300	excluding CUBA
Asia	13,162	19,711	12,032	17,833	excluding JAPAN
Africa	6,468	7,889	5,288	8,267	excluding SOUTH AFRICA

The contrast of wealth and poverty in Latin America's cities today:

slums and skyscrapers in Río de Janeiro

Economic development

At the root of Latin America's problems are economic difficulties. Only Mexico has so far achieved a soundly balanced economy, though forty years ago no one would have doubted Argentina's prospects. The United Nations Economics Commission for Latin America (ECLA) has estimated that if the purchasing power of Latin America's exports per head (excluding Venezuela, rich in oil) is taken as one hundred in 1928, it had fallen to thirty-seven by 1955, and thirty-two in 1965. Latin America has never recovered from the Depression because her share of the world's market in primary products, of which she was the greatest supplier in 1914, has fallen. The situation has been made worse by two factors: Africa is now an alternative source of supply for primary products; and the international trading and monetary systems have been too rigid to allow Latin American countries to change from being exporters of primary products to exporters of manufactured goods. Their problems have been further increased by internal inflation which has cancelled out any real growth in most states.

Latin America is therefore at the mercy of world forces which she cannot control. Only the rich countries can help her out of her present dilemma. Dr Prebisch has shown how countries which are dependent on the sale of primary commodities for their revenue are vulnerable to fluctuations in demand from the rich industrial nations. In a free market system, a decline in demand for such commodities harshly affects the primary producers, while an increase in the price of primary goods is not usually passed on to the supplying nation. The importers of primary products are the rich industrial nations. They do not want to pay more for these products than they need, and though there are international commodity agreements today, which exist to cushion both the rich and the poor nations against violent price fluctuations, they generally work in favour of the importing rather than the primary producing countries.

Attempts have been made to solve the dilemma. New commodity agreements have been signed which are more generous to the supplier, but the rich countries still hold the whip hand because they can control the prices of manufactured goods which the primary producers need to buy. In 1961 two attempts were made to establish a more integrated economy in Latin America by starting common markets. The CACM has succeeded in integrating the economies of the five Central American Republics, despite pessimistic forecasts. The Latin American Free Trade Area (LAFTA) has not been successful. The population of the member countries: Argentina, Bolivia, Brazil, Chile, Colombia, Ecuador, Mexico, Paraguay, Peru, Uruguay, and Venezuela constitute 90% of the population of Latin America, and include the most developed countries. The difficulties facing LAFTA were immense: rivalry between the most powerful states; fears from smaller countries of domination; the problems of making all economies compatible; and poor communications.

Trade between member countries did increase by well over 100% between 1961 and 1965. Much mutual suspicion and ignorance was overcome by frequent meetings of delegates from member states. But few states were able to increase their competitiveness in world markets, in the 1960s when commodity prices were declining still further.

Latin American countries could do something to strengthen their economies in certain ways: agriculture needs reforming in most states. Methods are backward and inefficient, crops are not marketed as cheaply as they could be, and food prices are too high. Properly controlled and organised agrarian reform, matched by technical change and financial investment in agriculture, could make Latin America a self sufficient region for foodstuffs. Protective tariffs which make industries artificially viable will also have to disappear. Tax reform leading to revenue being collected before inflation reduces its value by half. Finally, if the government payroll in the service industries could be reduced, their could be further capital investment in new industries and housing schemes, which would also appease the growing social discontent of the urban masses.

It is nevertheless difficult to avoid the conclusion that whatever Latin Americans do for themselves, it is the rich nations of the world which hold the key to their future.

DATES AND EVENTS

1492	Christopher Columbus reached the New World.
1519–1521	Hernán Cortes conquered Mexico.
1531–1535	Francisco Pizarro conquered Peru.
1804	Haiti gained independence from France, the first colony in Latin America to be freed.
1808	Napoleon Bonaparte usurped power in Spain.
1810–1828	All Spanish America except Cuba became free.
1822	Brazil threw off Portuguese rule; Brazilian empire set up.
1844	Dominican Republic freed from Haiti
1846–1847	War between Mexico and the United States
1865–1870	The War of the Triple Alliance
1879–1883	The War of the Pacific
1889	The Brazilian Empire replaced by a republic
1898–1899	The Spanish-American War
1902	Cuba gained independence from Spain.
1903	Panama gained independence from Colombia.
1903	José Batlle began to establish a welfare state in Uruguay.
1910	A social revolution began in Mexico.
1916	The first radical proclaimed president in Argentina.
1920	The first real challenge to aristocratic ascendancy in Chile.
1929–1931	The Great Depression had serious effects in Latin America.
1930	Getúlio Vargas began to rule in Brazil.
1932–1935	The Chaco War
1944–1954	A social revolution in Guatemala
1946	Juan Perón began to rule in Argentina.
1952	A social revolution was begun in Bolivia.
1958	Fidel Castro began the most profound revolution in Latin America since that of Mexico in 1910.
1962	The Cuban missile crisis
1970	A Marxist government elected in Chile

GLOSSARY

ALTIPLANO   the high plateau of the Andes, especially in Bolivia and Peru

AUDIENCIA   a legal body in Spanish America which also had considerable political power.

AYLLU   the smallest unit in the Inca Empire, resembling an English village

BANANA REPUBLICS   a term normally used in disparagement to describe the traditional dependence of the Central American Republics on banana exports

CABILDO   a town council in colonial America; this was the only administrative body on which creoles might sometimes sit.

CAUDILLO   a chief or leader with a military training who establishes control over part or all of a country; he first emerged after the Wars of Independence.

CONQUISTADOR   term applied to the conquerors of Spanish America

CONSULADO   a merchant guild; e.g. the consulado at Seville

CORTES   a legislative assembly or parliament in Spain and Portugal

CREOLE (Spanish: CRIOLLO)   a white settler in the Spanish colonies, generally excluded from political power, but dominating the economy of colonial life by controlling, for example, agriculture and mining

DESCAMISADOS   'the shirtless ones'—followers of Juan Perón

DONATORIOS   the Portuguese leaders who were given wide powers to establish and settle twelve colonies in Brazil in 1533.

EJIDO   the agricultural land held in common by the members of a village in Aztec Mexico; many ejidos were taken over by encomenderos after the Spanish Conquest, but should have been revived under the terms of the 1917 Constitution. The land redistribution which took place led to the creation of small peasant holdings and cooperatives rather than the original ejidos.

ENCOMENDERO   a Spanish settler in the New World, given a title to lands and control over Indians on those lands

ENCOMIENDA   a title to lands granted by the Spanish crown to encomenderos, but not awarded after 1542, following criticism of the treatment of Indians

ESTANCIA   a farm or ranch controlled by its estanciero or landowner; the term usually applied to farms in Argentina, Chile and Uruguay. Elsewhere the term hacienda is more common.

FAZENDA   a plantation in Brazil; hence FAZENDIERO, a planter

FRIGORÍFICO   a cold meat packing plant

GAUCHO   a cowboy of the Argentine and Uruguayan pampa; the traditional gaucho wished to be free from political control from the city. A number of gaucho leaders emerged as successful caudillos after independence.

HACIENDA   a ranch controlled by a HACENDADO, or landowner

JUNTAS   assemblies set up in Spain and in the colonies after Napoleon's entry into Spain in 1808; they were established in the name of Ferdinand VII, who had been forced to renounce the throne, but became in Spanish America a catalyst for independence. The term is also used to describe a faction or clique who seize power.

LLANOS   the plains of Venezuela, traditionally ruled by LLANEROS or cowboys

MAMELUCOS   mestizo adventurers who extended Brazil's frontiers westwards in the seventeenth century.

MESTIZOS   people of mixed Spanish and Indian blood

MILPAS   maize fields in Central America

MULATOS   people of mixed white and Negro blood

PAMPA   plains of Argentina

PENINSULARES   a term used to describe the Spaniards who were employed in the colonies as administrators and officials, as opposed to the Spanish settlers, the creoles.

PORTEÑOS   a citizen of the port—a term applied to the citizens of Buenos Aires

QUIPU   a series of knotted strings which were used by the Incas for recording information. They did not have a written language.

YERBA MATÉ   a tea produced by putting the leaves from the yerba tree into a gourd and covering them with boiling water. The drink is then infused through a metal straw. Maté is the traditional drink in Paraguay, Argentina and Uruguay.

ZAMBOS   people of mixed Indian and Negro blood

BIBLIOGRAPHY

Some suggested titles for further reading:

Bushnell, G. H. S.: *The First Americans*, Thames and Hudson, 1968
Coe, M. D.: *The Maya*, Thames and Hudson, 1966
Mason, J. A.: *The Ancient Civilisations of Peru*, Penguin Books, 1957
Vaillant, G. C.: *The Aztecs of Mexico*, Penguin Books, 1964

Diaz, B., translated and edited by J. M. Cohen: *The Conquest of New Spain*, Penguin Books, 1963
Gibson, C.: *Spain in America*, Harper and Row, New York, 1966
Parry, J. H.: *The Age of Reconnaissance 1450-1650*, Weidenfeld and Nicolson, 1963
Prescott, W. H.: *History of the Conquest of Peru*, Allen and Unwin, 1959
de Zarate, A, translated and edited by J. M. Cohen: *The Discovery and Conquest of Peru*, Penguin Books, 1968

Benham, F. and Holley, H.: *A short introduction to the economy of Latin America*, Oxford University Press, 1960
Blakemore, H.: *Latin America*, Oxford University Press, 1966
Draper, T.: *Castro's Revolution: Myths and Realities*, Thames and Hudson, 1962
Humphreys, R. A.: *The evolution of modern Latin America*, Oxford University Press, 1946
Johnson, J. J.: *Political Change in Latin America: the Emergence of the Middle Sectors*, Stanford, 1958
Lieuwen, E.: *Arms and Politics in Latin America*, Oxford University Press, 1964
Pendle, G.: *A History of Latin America*, Penguin Books, 1963
Schneider, R. and Kingsbury, R.: *An Atlas of Latin American Affairs*, Methuen, 1966

Conrad, J.: *Nostromo*, Penguin Books, 1963
Guiraldes, R., translated by H. de Onis: *Don Segundo Sombra*, New English Library, 1966
Huxley, A.: *Beyond the Mexique Bay*, Penguin Books, 1955
Meyer, G.: *The River and the People*, Methuen, 1965

INDEX

INDEX